Contents

Preface

For every Christian a pilgrimage to the Holy Land should truly be the journey of a lifetime. To visit the country in which Jesus was born, proclaimed his Gospel, was crucified, and overcame the power of death is not only a privilege but at the very least must be a gateway to a fuller understanding of his teaching. The greatest insight is perhaps in actually seeing some of the things that Jesus saw and to relate many of his sayings to the background in which they were spoken. The experience often brings about a strengthening of faith and a desire to return to the land which has had such a profound influence upon mankind.

The purpose of this guide book is: (a) to provide some background knowledge about each site together with details of how to reach it on foot or by car; (b) to explain the site's main features in a 'guide-yourself' form; (c) to supply some practical information on the facilities available. Included where appropriate is an excerpt from one of the four Gospels describing the event which occurred at, or very near, the shrine which now commemorates the occasion. A full list of Gospel references is given at the end of the book.

We are encouraged that our first attempt at compiling a practical guide has proved so helpful to many thousands of pilgrims. However in previously restricting ourselves to Gospel sites, a number of important places of general interest like Masada had to be omitted. In this completely revised edition we have added eleven extra places which might be included in a pilgrimage itinerary, whilst still retaining the guide's useful pocket size.

A pilgrimage to the Holy Land is often the fulfilment of a lifetime's ambition and it is therefore important to ensure that the very best use is made of the precious time available. Our hope is that this book will provide exactly the right balance of background knowledge and practical information in an easily accessible format.

Norman Wareham
Jill Gill

AUTHORS' NOTES

The text for each site opens with a brief description and usually ends with our personal comments.

Most of the chosen Gospel readings are from the Revised English Bible (1990), but in instances where it was felt that the passage in the Authorised Version (1611) is more familiar this has been selected. Each reading is followed by a few lines from a hymn which are offered as a prayerful thought.

The sections are arranged in a geographical sequence, but a comprehensive index at the end enables immediate reference to each individual site.

The general information supplied – in particular opening/closing times and telephone numbers – has been carefully checked at the time of writing, but inevitably some details may vary from time to time.

Only sketch maps are included in this guide on the assumption that most pilgrims will have received detailed maps from their tour agency.

Acknowledgements

We would like to express our sincere appreciation to the following for their help in the preparation of this guide:

McCabe Travel London; The Israel Government Tourist Office London; Albina Tours Jerusalem; Mohammed Joulani Jerusalem.

We should once again like to thank Terence Gill for drawing up the maps and plans, and Michael Sampson for his delightful line drawings.

USEFUL INFORMATION

ESSENTIALS

Visitors to Israel must possess a full ten-year passport which should be valid for at least six months after the planned return date. Visas are not required for British passport holders.

Travel Insurance is essential especially to cover medical emergencies as costs can be very high.

Vaccinations and inoculations are no longer necessary, but if you have any doubt, it would be wise to seek medical advice.

FACTS ABOUT ISRAEL

The Land itself

The country is surprisingly small – not much larger in area than Wales. The distance from Jerusalem to the Sea of Galilee is less than 100 miles.

The majority of the Gospel sites are easily accessible and are mainly confined within three comparatively small areas: Jerusalem, Nazareth and Galilee.

Clocks in Israel are normally two hours ahead of Britain.

English is widely spoken. In tourist areas most notices and road signs are in Hebrew, Arabic and English.

General information and maps can be obtained from the Israel Government Tourist Office, 18 Great Marlborough Street, London, W1V 1AF. Tel: 0171-434 3651. Fax: 0171-437 0527.

Climate

Temperatures vary enormously and the mean annual rainfall is almost equal to that of London but most of it falls between mid-November and mid-March. Sunset is within a narrow time-band throughout the year: 18.00–19.30 (timings are different during the adjusted 'Summertime'). There is very little twilight.

The most popular times with British visitors are between April and mid-June, or late September to mid-November when the temperatures are not oppressive. Summer is generally hot, but Winter can be surprisingly cold and particularly in Jerusalem, 2,500 feet (760 metres) above sea level, where night-frosts and even snow are not uncommon.

The following table of average daily fahrenheit temperatures has been supplied by the Israel Government Tourist Office. However it should be remembered that evenings in Jerusalem can be quite chilly during Spring and Autumn. The Jordan Valley/Dead Sea

area is consistently warm or very hot, while Tiberias is always much warmer than Jerusalem with some degree of humidity.

	Jan	Feb	Mar	Apl	May	Jne	Jly	Aug	Spt	Oct	Nov	Dec
Jerusalem:	53.0	57.4	60.8	69.4	77.4	81.3	85.3	85.5	81.9	77.9	66.6	56.1
Tiberias:	64.9	67.1	72.3	80.1	89.1	94.8	97.9	98.8	95.0	89.2	78.3	68.2
Dead Sea:	68.9	71.6	77.9	89.2	92.3	99.1	102.1	101.7	96.4	89.6	80.6	71.8

Finance

Banking Hours: Sunday, Tuesday, Thursday: 8.30–12.30 16.00–
18.00
Monday and Wednesday: 8.30–12.30
Friday and eve of Jewish Holy Days: 8.30–12.00

The shekel (NIS) is divided into 100 agorots. Sterling and dollar notes are welcomed, but change will be given in shekels. Visa, Access, American Express and Diners Club cards are accepted by most of the larger hotels and businesses. Traveller's cheques are also accepted. Banks are often difficult to find in and around the Old City of Jerusalem, but there are plenty of money-changers who offer a good rate of exchange for cash or Traveller's cheques.

GENERAL ADVICE

Clothing

Mid-November to mid-March: Ordinary light Winter garments and footwear; raincoats and umbrellas.
Late March and April: Light Spring clothing but a woolly will often be required in Jerusalem during the cool evenings.
May to mid-October: Very light casual clothing and comfortable footwear. Sun hat and sunglasses are essential as the light is very dazzling.
Late October to mid-November: Dress as for March/April, but it can be warmer in the Autumn than in the Spring.

Medical

Favoured medicines are best purchased before departure and should be clearly labelled.

All emergency treatment, doctor's visits and prescriptions have to be paid for at the time, so allow sufficient funds. Insurance companies will wish to see receipts.

Stomach upsets are very common. During the hot months it is most important to drink plenty – and often – to avoid the very deal danger of dehydration. A small vacuum flask might prove useful. Sunburn and blisters can also be a problem for the unwary visitor.

Mains water is normally safe, but if you have a delicate stomach you are strongly advised to purchase bottled water. All drinks in hotels are fairly expensive. Tea/coffee making facilities are not normally provided in bedrooms.

Electrical Equipment

Current is AC 220 volts, 50 cycles. The Israeli sockets are usually small three-pronged but not of English or European design. A travelplug adaptor will be necessary. Airlines require electrical equipment to be carried in hand luggage.

A pocket torch will also be useful in some ancient sites where lighting is poor. Take sufficient films and batteries for your photographic needs because these can be fairly expensive in Israel.

The Three Monotheistic Faiths

It should be remembered that Jerusalem is a religious centre for Jews, Muslims and Christians. The three 'Holy Days' can therefore cause some confusion! Friday for Muslims; Saturday for Jews; and Sunday for Christians, when their respective shops are closed. The Jews start their Sabbath ('Shabbat') at sunset on Friday when all public transport operated by them ceases.

In Mosques and Churches visitors are required to dress modestly. Ladies should ensure that their shoulders and upper arms are covered – a light shawl would be useful for this purpose. Anyone in shorts will be refused admission.

Souvenirs

Consider bringing home leather goods, olive wood carvings, mother of pearl items, diamond jewellery, copperware, embroidered clothes and linen, ceramics, dried fruits, nuts, herbs and spices. Tax can be reclaimed on the more expensive items when leaving the country but relevant receipts must be presented.

The Tourist 'Green Card'

This allows 14 days unlimited admission to 43 National Parks Authority sites, mostly of archaeological interest, of which eight are covered in this book. For those planning their own itinerary it may be worth purchasing and is available from the National Parks Authority headquarters in Tel-Aviv (4 Rav Alluf M. Makleff Street, Hakirya, 61070 Tel-Aviv.) POB 7028. Tel: (03) 6952281. Fax: (03) 6967643, or the ticket office at many of their sites.

JERUSALEM
Particular advice

Visitors should be particularly careful in the jostling crowds of the Old City to ensure that purses and wallets are not accessible to pickpockets and bag snatchers.

Fruit is plentiful but should be thoroughly washed. Be wary of purchasing pressed orange juice – or any other unpackaged consumable – in the street.

Transport

The larger taxis, known as 'sheruts', seat seven passengers. Be prepared to share, but always agree a price before departure. Taxi ranks are to be found at the Damascus and Jaffa Gates.

Bus Stations

Arab: (1) Opposite the City walls between Damascus and Herod's Gates: To Mount of Olives No. 75; Bethlehem 23; Bethany 36; Jericho 28.

(2) Opposite Garden Tomb (Nablus Road): To El-Qubeibah 45; Jacob's Well 62.

Israeli: Pick up near Jaffa Gate ('Egged' Buses): To Ein Kerim 17; Abu Gosh 185; Yad Vashem 20.

EMERGENCIES

British Embassy. 192 Hayarkon Street, Tel Aviv. Tel: (03) 5249171. Fax: (03) 5243313.

British Consulate. Sheikh Jarrah Quarter: Nashashibi Street, East Jerusalem. Tel: (02) 828281. Fax: (02) 322368.

Emergency Services: **Police** 100 **Medical** 101 **Fire** 102

To dial England: 00-44 – then the full UK number without the first '0'

USEFUL ADDRESSES FOR THE PILGRIM

Christian Information Centre run by the Franciscans who administer the majority of the Gospel sites. Enter the Old City by the Jaffa Gate, follow the Citadel walls around to the right and the entrance is almost opposite the bridge crossing the moat. A great deal of useful information is available here including the times of Religious Services and also the language in which each is conducted. Bus timetables; current opening times of the sites; churches; mosques; and other places of interest, together with details of any special attractions are also available.
Open: 8.30–13.00. Closed on Sundays and holidays.
POB 14308, Jerusalem. Tel: (02) 272692. Fax: (02) 286417.

Tourist Information Office. Just inside the Jaffa Gate, on the left, in the Old City. POB 97911. Tel: (02) 280382.
Open: Sun–Thur: 8.30–18.00. Friday 8.30–14.00. Closed Saturday.

CHRISTIAN PERIODS AND DEVELOPMENT

Explanation of the terminology used in the text:

Second Temple Period: 37 BC to AD 70. During this period King Herod the Great's magnificent building – so familiar to Jesus – was constructed. Strictly speaking, his Temple was the third because the second, erected on a much smaller scale, came into being after the return of the Jews from exile in Babylon circa 587 BC.

Judeo/Christian: A term used to describe the period between The Resurrection and the construction of the first purpose-built churches. During these three centuries the early Christians continued to worship in their synagogues and in house groups.

Constantinian: A definition applied to the very first churches to be built in the Holy Land on the specific instructions of the Roman Emperor Constantine (c.274–337) following his conversion to Christianity by his mother, St Helena.

Byzantine: A rather loose term to describe the churches built during the seven centuries which elapsed between the death of Constantine and the arrival of the Crusaders in the eleventh century. Most were totally destroyed by the Persians in AD 614 after which Christianity sank to a low ebb. However the Church of the Nativity in Bethlehem survived, and the Church of the Holy Sepulchre in Jerusalem was twice rebuilt on a modest scale.

Crusader: 1096–1187. An incredibly industrious period of building and reconstruction during a span of less than one hundred years. Many of their churches were built upon the ruins of Byzantine foundations. Although the Crusaders were defeated in battle by Saladin in 1187, they continued to control the Port of Acre until 1291.

Middle Ages: Following the Crusader period the Muslims became the predominant influence throughout Palestine. However as Jesus is acknowledged as a prophet by the Islamic faith they were not altogether intolerant of the followers of Christ. In consequence some churches survived and were occupied during the Middle Ages by Christian monastic communities from all over Europe – in the main, the Augustinians, Benedictines and Franciscans.

Modern Times: Towards the end of the nineteenth century there was a marked increase in Christian missionary activity and a number of churches were built, some on Crusader and Byzantine foundations. During the first half of the twentieth century there was a great upsurge in Christian activity and a considerable number of Arabs, particularly in Bethlehem, East Jerusalem, and Nazareth, were converted to the faith.

Since the inauguration of the State of Israel many churches have been built or renovated. Thanks to the ease of modern travel, large numbers of pilgrims continue to flock to the Holy Land from all over the world.

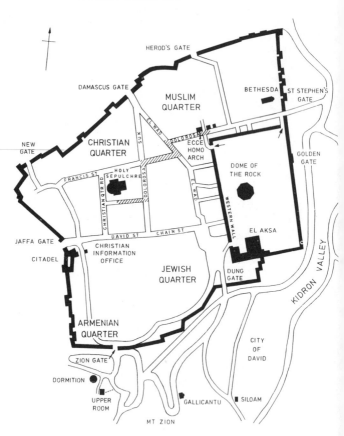

JERUSALEM OLD CITY

Jerusalem

One of the most ancient cities in the world, Jerusalem holds the unique distinction of being the 'Holy City' for half the human race – for Jews, Christians, and Muslims. During the course of its long and turbulent history the City has been besieged on more than fifty occasions, conquered thirty-six times, and has suffered no less than ten total destructions.

These simple statements sum up the importance of this relatively small community which has played such an important role in the history of mankind.

Today it is difficult to realise that less than 150 years ago there were no houses outside the Old City walls. Even by the end of the British Mandate in 1948 Jerusalem had not developed extensively. However since the six-day war in 1967 there has been a tremendous growth which continues at a phenomenal pace. On the Judaean hills where previously shepherds tended their sheep, have sprung up the Israeli Parliament and other government buildings, an extensive University, the National Museum, and a number of tall hotels which now dominate the skyline. Furthermore, the City has recently been surrounded by large urban residential developments, some of which border on to the desert. An idea of the size of modern Jerusalem can be obtained from the high ground along the road to Bethlehem.

As can be seen from the plan opposite the Old City today is divided into four distinct quarters – in addition to the Temple Area which stands on its own and occupies most of the eastern boundary. Working clockwise from the Jaffa Gate:

The Christian Quarter: In the north-west corner. This sector is roughly bounded by the road running east from the Jaffa Gate and south from the Damascus Gate. Within the area is the Church of the Holy Sepulchre, and the residences of the Coptic, Greek Catholic, Greek Orthodox, and Roman Catholic Patriarchs. Many other Christian communities are also represented including the Abyssinians, Lutherans, Russian Orthodox, and the Knights Hospitalers.

The Muslim Quarter: In the north-east corner. Roughly bounded by the road running south from the Damascus Gate as far as the road continuing east from the Jaffa Gate. Of particular Christian interest within this area is the Pool of Bethesda and the

Crusader Church of St Anne, the Roman Catholic Seminary of the Flagellation, the Convent of the Sisters of Zion, and also part of the Via Dolorosa.

The Jewish Quarter: Situated in the south, but west of the large plaza in front of the Western Wall of the Temple Area. Most of this sector was demolished after 1967 and rebuilt in sympathy with the original architecture. Bordering on this area is the Church of St Mark which the Assyrians claim is built over the site of the 'Upper Room'.

The Armenian Quarter: This somewhat exclusive sector lies directly to the west of the modern Jewish Quarter and reaches as far as the western walls of the City. Within it is the Cathedral of St James and the residence of the Armenian Patriarch. To the north of this – before completing the circuit and reaching the Jaffa Gate – is the Citadel which occupies the site of Herod's Palace. Opposite the drawbridge is the entrance to Christ Church, the only Anglican church within the Old City.

The present walls were in the main built by Suleiman the Magnificent in the sixteenth century and in them are eight gates: Jaffa Gate in the west; New Gate, Damascus Gate and Herod's Gate in the north; St Stephen's Gate and the Golden Gate (sealed for several centuries) in the east; while in the southern walls are the Dung Gate and Zion Gate.

To walk around the top of the walls is a rewarding experience and provides an excellent orientation. Access can be obtained from the Damascus and Jaffa Gates and about two-thirds of the total circumference is open to the public. Many of the buildings in the Old City, and in particular the covered 'Suqs' (markets), were constructed by the Crusaders and therefore date from the twelfth century.

A Brief History

The earliest Biblical record (Genesis 14.18) is from the time of Abraham, circa 2,000 BC, when reference was made to the habitation known as 'Salem', the Hebrew word for peace. Many scholars consider that this was an abbreviated form of Jerusalem. There is also a strong tradition that Mount Moriah – upon which Abraham prepared to sacrifice his son Isaac in obedience to God – is the same mount on which were later built the Temples of Solomon, Herod, and the present Dome of the Rock.

Principal Dates

1000 BC	*King David*	captured the city from the Jebusites.
965	*King Solomon,*	David's son, built the first Temple.

587	*King Nebuchadnezzar* captured the city, destroyed the Temple and carried off the Jews to exile in Babylon.
538	The Jews returned and a smaller Temple was rebuilt.
332	*Alexander the Great* captured the city.
167	*The Hasmonean Kings* allowed the Jews independence.
63	*The Romans* captured the city.
37	*Herod the Great* was appointed King. The city was beautified and the Temple rebuilt on a magnificent scale.

The Birth of Jesus

AD 70	*Titus* the Roman Emperor, totally destroyed the city including the Temple following a Jewish revolt.
135	*Hadrian* after crushing a second Jewish revolt, rebuilt the city as a typical Roman provincial town and renamed it 'Aelia Capitolina'. The Jews were forbidden entry on penalty of death.
330	*Constantine* the Roman Emperor, was converted to Christianity by his mother, St Helena. He built four principal churches: The Church of the Holy Sepulchre; 'Eleona' on the Mount of Olives; a church on Mount Zion; and the Church of the Nativity in Bethlehem.
614	*The Persians* conquered the Holy Land and destroyed all its churches with the exception of the Church of the Nativity in Bethlehem.
636	*The Muslim Arabs* gained control and held authority for nearly 500 years.
1099	The Crusaders captured the city and built many churches.
1187	*Saladin*, the Muslim leader, defeated the Crusaders.
1517	*The Turks* captured the city and remained in control for the next 400 years.
1917	*General Allenby* took possession of the city. Palestine came under mandatory British control with the authority of the League of Nations.

| 1948 | *The United Nations* at the end of British control, partitioned the country between Israel and Jordan. A year later the state of Israel was inaugurated. |
| 1967 | The Six Day War between Arabs and |

Jews resulted in the Israeli occupation of the 'West Bank' and the 'Gaza Strip'. The city is no longer arbitrarily divided and the Jews are able to worship once again at the Western Wall.

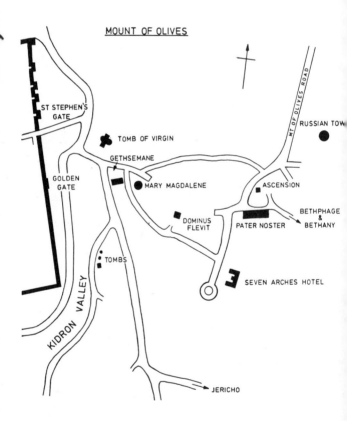

Mount of Olives

The Place of the Ascension
The Church of the Pater Noster
Dominus Flevit

The Mount is the high ground rising above the Kidron Valley to the east of the Old City. Sometimes known as 'Olivet', it is a Gospel site in its own right and there are many New Testament references to it. St Luke records that it was from here that Jesus wept over the City as he foretold its destruction.

In addition to the three sites described in detail below, mention should be made of the slender tower on its summit which is part of the Russian Orthodox Convent of the Ascension from where there are magnificent views. Unfortunately the tower is rarely open to the public.

* * *

THE PLACE OF THE ASCENSION

A small octagonal shrine at the top of the Mount of Olives built over the place where, according to tradition, Jesus ascended into heaven. St Luke, the writer of the Acts of the Apostles, mentions that the Disciples came down from the Mount of Olives after the Ascension.

Access (see map opposite)

1. *On foot:* From St Stephen's Gate (also known as the Lion Gate) on the east side of the Old City, walk down the hill for 200 metres and turn right into the main Jericho Road. Continue to the bottom of the Kidron Valley until reaching the stone wall surrounding the Church of All Nations in the Garden of Gethsemane. Take the narrow road to the left of the wall and keep straight on up the steep hill for about 500 metres until reaching the road running north/south along the top of the Mount of Olives. Here turn to the right, pass the Mount of Olives Hotel and shortly after, on the left, will be seen the octagonal minaret of a mosque adjacent to the site. Allow a good half hour to reach the shrine.

2. *By car:* The route above is also possible, but there is no point in starting from St Stephen's Gate because it is at the end of a narrow cul-de-sac. Follow the City walls round from the Damascus Gate until reaching the Garden of Gethsemane at the bottom of the Kidron Valley, then drive up the steep hill mentioned above.

Details

Wide steps lead up to the site which is owned by the Muslims and if closed it may be necessary to seek admission from the custodian of the mosque.

The earliest church here was built by Pomenia, a wealthy Roman lady, at the end of the fourth century, but this was destroyed by the Persians in AD 614. A little later Bishop Modestus erected a circular building which was open to the skies and it is recorded that eight lamps shone brilliantly at night through the windows so that they could be seen from the City.

The existing structure is basically Crusader. In 1102 they erected an impressive shrine comprising an outer colonnaded cloister within which stood an octagon of slender columns and arches open to the sky. On the defeat of the Crusaders the Muslims added a cupola to the central octagon and filled-in the arches with stone blocks. The fine carved capitals are worth closer inspection. The encircling cloister was destroyed and the east wall re-aligned. The shrine today is a mere shadow of its previous splendour.

Within the structure is a rock upon which there is an indentation – dubiously reputed to be Christ's right footprint. It is worth remembering that Jesus is honoured by the Muslims as a Prophet – they are unable to accept the Crucifixion or the Resurrection, but they acknowledge the Ascension.

Annually, on the Feast of the Ascension the Armenian, Coptic, Greek Orthodox, Roman Catholic, and Syrian Churches are each allowed to celebrate Mass within the

---

The Ascension (Luke 24. 50–52)

Jesus led the disciples out as far as to Bethany, and he lifted up his hands, and blessed them. And it came to pass, while he blessed them, he was parted from them, and carried up into heaven. (AV)

'All praise to thee who art gone up triumphantly to heaven;
All praise to God the Father's name and Holy Ghost be given.'

For further Gospel references, see page 195

compound. The metal rings high up on the outer walls enable protective awnings to be erected above temporary altars.

Authors' Comments

It is not surprising that many pilgrims find this to be a somewhat bizarre site – more of a curiosity than a holy place.

Opening times: Ring the bell

Souvenir Shop: A limited number of souvenirs beside the shrine

Toilets: None

Custodian: The Muslims. There is a small admission fee

*   *   *

THE CHURCH OF THE PATER NOSTER

OUR FATHER

Here on the Mount of Olives, according to tradition, Jesus taught his Disciples 'The Lord's Prayer'. Within the grounds of the French Carmelite Convent are the four-metre high walls of an uncompleted church. Below the altar are the few remaining ruins of the 'Eleona' Basilica built in the fourth century by the Emperor Constantine.

Access

The Church and Convent lie at the junction of the roads which run north/south and east/west over the Mount of Olives (*see access instructions for the Place of the Ascension on page 5*). Pater Noster is 100 metres further along the road from that site. Allow a good half an hour to walk from St Stephen's Gate.

Tour

From the entrance gate descend the three short flights of steps which lead down into the uncompleted Church. Mounted on the wall, immediately to the left, is a white limestone plaque upon which the Lord's Prayer is inscribed in Aramaic and ancient Hebrew. Below the modern altar platform, steps lead down to the somewhat scanty remains of the 'Eleona' Basilica (Greek: 'Olive Tree'). This was one of the four original churches built in the Holy Land on the orders of the Emperor Constantine in AD 330. The others were the Church of the Holy Sepulchre; a Church on Mount Zion; and the Church of the Nativity in Bethlehem.

7

Below the altar platform the apse of the crypt of the original Basilica is clearly visible and this was partially built within a cave. In addition to commemorating the place where Jesus taught the Disciples his own prayer, there is also a tradition that near here he spoke to them of the destruction of Jerusalem and the nature of the coming Kingdom. At the back of the ancient crypt there are some first century AD tombs.

The Basilica was destroyed by the Persians in AD 614. In the twelfth century the Crusaders built another church on the site, but after their defeat the ruins were occupied by the Muslims.

In 1868 the land was bought by the Princess de la Tour d'Auvergne who erected the present Convent with its cloister for the Carmelite Sisters. In 1918 the French launched an appeal to build a new Basilica dedicated to the Sacred Heart. Work commenced in 1920, but funds ran out and today the unfinished church remains open to the skies.

The Lord's Prayer is inscribed on the walls of the cloister, and more recently on the walls of the Church, in over 60 different languages. The English translation can be found by passing through the small doorway on the south side of the uncompleted church, turning left up the steps, and then following the cloister round to a vestibule on the right. It is interesting to

---

The Lord's Prayer (Matt 6. 7–15)

Jesus said, 'When ye pray, use not vain repetitions, as the heathen do: for they think that they shall be heard for their much speaking. Be not ye therefore like unto them: for your Father knoweth what things ye have need of before ye ask him. After this manner therefore pray ye:

Our Father which art in heaven, Hallowed be thy name. Thy kingdom come. Thy will be done in earth, as it is in heaven. Give us this day our daily bread: and forgive us our debts, as we forgive our debtors. And lead us not into temptation, but deliver us from evil: For thine is the kingdom, and the power, and the glory, for ever. Amen.

For if ye forgive men their trespasses, your heavenly Father will also forgive you. But if ye forgive not men their trespasses, neither will your Father forgive your trespasses'. (AV)

'"Forgive our sins as we forgive"
you taught us, Lord, to pray;
But you alone can grant us grace
to live the words we say.'

For further Gospel references, see page 197

see how one ceramic tile has been changed in order to conform with modern grammar: 'which art in heaven' has now been amended to 'who art in heaven'. Adjacent to this vestibule can be seen the tomb of the Princess de la Tour d'Auvergne.

Authors' Comments

An obvious place in which to say the Lord's Prayer but also – because the Church is on the Mount of Olives and open to the skies – a suitable site in which to call to mind Our Lord's Ascension into heaven.

Opening Times:
8.30–11.45 15.00–16.45
Closed Sundays

Souvenir Shop: Inside the entrance gate on the left

Toilets: None

Custodian: The French Carmelite Sisters

Telephone: (02) 894904

track road which rises to the right immediately behind the Church of All Nations. Allow about twelve minutes walking.

2. *From the top of the Mount of Olives:* Take the road which runs from north to south, and between the Convent of Pater Noster and the Seven Arches Hotel, steps lead down beside the Tombs of the Prophets – Haggai, Malachi, and Zechariah. From here allow about five minutes to descend the steps and steep path to the site.

Tour

From the entrance gate the path leads through flowering shrubs to the little Church which was built in 1955 to a design by the Italian Architect Antonio Barluzzi. At the end of the path bear left (to avoid passing in front of the altar window and obstructing the view from inside) and walk down to the terrace from

*   *   *

DOMINUS FLEVIT

THE LORD WEPT

A small tear-drop shaped Church halfway up the Mount of Olives which commemorates the occasion when Jesus wept over the City and foretold its destruction.

Access

1. *From Gethsemane:* The approach is via a steep single-

where there are magnificent views of the Temple Area and the Old City across the Kidron Valley.

To the north side of the Church are traces of earlier Byzantine and Crusader buildings. Before entering the doorway notice on the ground to the left a fine fifth century mosaic. The outstanding feature of this lovely little Church is the 'Chalice' window which frames, very movingly, the City beyond. The mosaic on the front of the altar is of a hen gathering her chicks under her wings as mentioned in St Luke's Gospel: 13.34. The Latin inscription on the wall is also from St Luke recording how Jesus wept over the City before entering Jerusalem on Palm Sunday. Notice on the floor at the back how the apse of an earlier church followed the Christian tradition of facing east rather than west. Some of the mosaics from this building are also incorporated in the modern floor.

On returning to the site entrance notice on the left, before reaching the gate, the ancient tomb complex containing sarcophagi and ossuaries which date from circa the second century BC to the fourth century AD.

Authors' Comments

The site is a very suitable place for meditation because it overlooks so much that is mentioned in the Gospel narrative.

Opening Times: 8.00–12.00 14.30–17.00 daily

Souvenir Shop: None

Toilets: To the left of the terrace

Custodian: The Franciscans.

Telephone: (02) 274931

Jesus weeps over the City (Luke 19. 41–44)

When Jesus came in sight of the city, he wept over it and said, 'If only you had known this day the way that leads to peace! But no; it is hidden from your sight. For a time will come upon you, when your enemies will set up siege-works against you; they will encircle you and hem you in at every point; they will bring you to the ground, you and your children within your walls, and not leave you one stone standing on another, because you did not recognize the time of God's visitation.' (REB)

'O pray for the peace of Jerusalem:
they shall prosper that love thee.'

Gethsemane

The Church of The Agony
The Cave of the Olive Press
The Tomb of the Virgin Mary
The Church of St Mary Magdalene
The Kidron Valley

Access *(see map on page 4)*

Gethsemane is situated in the Kidron Valley outside the eastern wall of the Temple Area. From St Stephen's Gate, also known as the Lion Gate, proceed down the hill for about 200 metres and turn right into the main Jericho Road. Bear round to the left and the Church of the Agony is ahead. Allow eight minutes walking.

*   *   *

THE CHURCH OF THE AGONY

Commonly called the Church of All Nations, whose striking west facade consists of a colonnaded portico with a fine mosaic above. Inside the Church is a bare rock upon which, according to tradition, Jesus prayed before his arrest on Maundy Thursday night. On the north side of the Church is a walled garden containing eight very ancient olive trees.

Tour

The entrance gate is 50 metres along the narrow road to the left of the wall protecting the ancient olive trees. Once inside, turn right to circumvent the garden. The largest of the trees has a girth of over 18 feet. It is impossible to date them specifically although in 1982 the University of California carried out carbon-dating tests the results of which indicate that some of the wood may be 2,300 years old.

Proceed around the garden to the portico of the west facade and enter the Church. Inside, the overall impression is one of quiet solemnity and this is greatly enhanced by the subdued violet-blue light coming through the alabaster windows. The focal point of the Church is the area of bedrock preserved in front of the main altar upon which it is claimed that Jesus prayed to his Father before his arrest. St Luke mentions that it was a 'stone's throw' from where the Disciples were sheltering and had fallen asleep. This is consistent with the proximity of the Cave of the Olive Press. The mosaic above the altar depicts the scene.

The iron wreath partially enclosing the rock represents the crown of thorns. Centrally, on three sides, a pair of thorn birds are featured in front of a Communion cup symbolising souls who wish to share the Chalice of Christ's passion. In each corner a silver dove is depicted caught in the thorns. The iron wreath was a gift from Australia.

Through a glass panel in the floor of the south aisle can be seen some original fourth century Byzantine mosaics which were part of the first church. The modern floor is an exact copy. The apses of the north and south aisles have been designed so as to incorporate some lower stone courses from this same early church which was reduced to ruins by the Persians in AD 614.

The Crusaders built another church on the site, but at an angle across the original foundations. Some remains of this twelfth century structure can be seen on the south side of the modern Basilica.

The present building, constructed on the line of the Byzantine foundations, was completed in 1924. Antonio Barluzzi, the Italian Architect, has succeeded in creating an atmosphere which reflects the anguish in the garden on that first Maundy Thursday night. The Basilica is often referred to as the 'Church of All Nations' because many countries contributed towards its cost. Their respective coats of arms are depicted in the twelve domes of the ceiling. Facing east, and working from the apses, on the left the cupolas represent: Argentina; Brazil; Chile; and Mexico. In the middle: Italy; France; Spain; and England. On the right: Belgium; Canada; Germany; and the United States. The mosaics in the apses were donated by Ireland, Hungary and Poland.

After leaving the Church, cross the main road and turn to admire the fine west facade. Surmounting the Corinthian columns are statues representing the four great evangelists: Matthew, Mark,

Luke and John. Above them is an inscription in Latin from Hebrews 5.7: 'Jesus offered up prayers and supplications, with loud cries and tears, (to him who was able to save him from death) and he was heard for his Godly fear'. The mosaic depicts Christ as the mediator between God and man on whose behalf He gives His very heart which an angel is shown receiving into his hands. To Christ's left there is a throng of lowly folk who, through their tears, look to him with confidence. To his right, the powerful and wise acknowledge the shortcomings of all their might and learning. On the summit the cross is flanked by two bronze stags.

The Agony, Betrayal and Arrest of Jesus (Luke 22. 39–54a)

Then Jesus went out and made his way as usual to the mount of Olives, accompanied by the disciples. When he reached the place he said to them, 'Pray that you may be spared the test.' He himself withdrew from them about a stone's throw, knelt down, and began to pray: 'Father, if it be your will, take this cup from me. Yet not my will but yours be done.' And now there appeared to him an angel from heaven bringing him strength, and in anguish of spirit he prayed the more urgently; and his sweat was like drops of blood falling to the ground.

When he rose from prayer and came to the disciples he found them asleep, worn out by grief. 'Why are you sleeping?' he said. 'Rise and pray that you may be spared the test.'

While he was still speaking a crowd appeared with the man called Judas, one of the Twelve, at their head. He came up to Jesus to kiss him; but Jesus said, 'Judas, would you betray the Son of Man with a kiss?' When his followers saw what was coming, they said, 'Lord, shall we use our swords?' And one of them struck at the high priest's servant, cutting off his right ear. But Jesus answered, 'Stop! No more of that!' Then he touched the man's ear and healed him.

Turning to the chief priests, the temple guards, and the elders, who had come to seize him, he said, 'Do you take me for a robber, that you have come out with swords and cudgels? Day after day, I have been with you in the temple, and you did not raise a hand against me. But this is your hour – when darkness reigns.' Then they arrested him and led him away.
(REB)

> 'Thine own disciple to the Jews has sold thee,
> With friendship's kiss and loyal word he came;
> How oft of faithful love my lips have told thee,
> While thou hast seen my falsehood and my shame.'

For further Gospel references, see page 197

13

Authors' Comments

Undoubtedly one of the most important Gospel sites in the Holy Land. Its devotional atmosphere makes a profound impression upon many pilgrims.

Opening Times:
8.00–12.00 14.30–18.00 daily
Winter: closes at 17.00

Souvenir Shop: None. (Beware of persistent street traders outside)

Toilets: None

Custodian: The Franciscans

Telephone: (02) 283264

* * *

THE CAVE OF THE OLIVE PRESS

Here, according to tradition, Jesus and his Disciples often sheltered.

Access

The Cave, and the entrance to the Tomb of the Virgin Mary, are to be found about 100 metres north from the facade of the Church of the Agony. Immediately behind the small domed monument to a fifteenth century Arab writer, descend the flight of steps leading down into a sunken courtyard. This was constructed in the twelfth century over an enormous water cistern. Ahead is the arched Crusader doorway to Mary's Tomb, but before entering it, take the narrow walled passageway to the right which leads to the Cave of the Olive Press.

Details

The Hebrew word *Gat Shemen*, from which the area derives its name, means olive press. Archaeological evidence has been found in the cave indicating that in Our Lord's time an olive press was situated in the recess where the altar now stands. Notice beneath it the bronze figures depicting two of the sleeping Disciples. At seasons other than harvest, the cave would have been used as a shelter and as such was known to Jesus and his followers. There is also evidence of Christian devotion here since the fourth century. Fragments of a mosaic floor and a pre-Christian water cistern can be seen at the back of the cave.

Authors' Comments

This site is often omitted from pilgrimage itineraries, which is a pity because here is a place which is basically unchanged and must have been familiar to Jesus.

Opening Times:
8.30–11.30 14.30–16.00 daily

Souvenir Shop: None

Toilets: None

Custodian: The Franciscans

Telephone: (02) 283264

The Franciscans were relieved of the custodianship of the shrine in 1857 and it is now used by the Eastern Orthodox Churches: the Armenians, Copts, Greeks, and Syrians. The Muslims are also allowed to worship here because they reverence Mary as the Mother of the Prophet Jesus. There is a mihrab (prayer niche) to the right of the tomb. The atmosphere is typical of Eastern Orthodox Churches and illumination is confined to bare electric light bulbs.

THE TOMB OF THE VIRGIN MARY

Sometimes referred to as the Church of the Assumption. The Crusader doorway gives access to a long flight of steps leading down into the crypt which is all that now remains of a fourth century church containing the reputed tomb of the Mother of Our Lord.

Access

See the Cave of the Olive Press opposite.

Tour

The plain arched Crusader entrance to the shrine is on the north side of the sunken courtyard. From the entrance door 44 steps lead down through the gloom to a dungeon-like crypt which is all that now remains of the original fourth century Byzantine Church. The crypt therefore is the oldest most complete religious building in Jerusalem, and this in itself justifies a visit.

At the bottom of the steps on the right is an altar behind which is an aedicule built over the reputed tomb of the Mother of Our Lord. It is not unlike that in the Church of the Holy Sepulchre except, in this instance, much of the original hewn rock still remains. The architect separated it from the adjoining rocky mass destroying other graves in the area. It is worth remembering that in the Turkish city of Ephesus there is another tomb claimed to be that of Mary. St John, into whose care Jesus entrusted his Mother, lived in that city towards the end of his life.

Hanging from the ceiling are a myriad of gold and silver lamps, while around the walls are many ikons and other religious paintings. The roof has been blackened over the centuries by the use of candles, and on the Feast of

15

the Assumption the whole appearance is enhanced by the light from hundreds of tapers carried by worshippers.

On ascending the marble steps towards the daylight notice, about halfway up on the right, a chapel dedicated to St Joseph, Mary's husband. On the left is another dedicated to her parents St Joachim and St Anne.

Authors' Comments

A typical Eastern Orthodox setting. Well worth a visit because of the antiquity of the site. Take a torch to illuminate the ikons and paintings.

Opening Times:
6.00–11.45 14.30–17.00 daily

Souvenir Shop: None

Toilets: None

Custodians:
The Greek Orthodox Church
A small donation is expected

*   *   *

THE CHURCH OF ST MARY MAGDALENE

An impressive Russian Orthodox Church on the rising ground behind the Church of the Agony and distinguished by its seven gold onion-shaped domes.

Access

Take the road to the right immediately behind the Church of the Agony. The entrance to the Convent is on the left.

Details

This distinctive Church was built in 1888 in a typical seventeenth century Russian style by Czar Alexander III in memory of his mother. Visitors are only allowed to view the interior from the back of the nave, but a number of nineteenth century paintings and ikons can be seen. Outside, there is a splendid view from the terrace across the Kidron Valley to the eastern wall of the Temple Area. Within the garden is buried Princess Alice of Greece, Mother of HRH Prince Philip, Duke of Edinburgh.

Authors' Comments

The exterior of the Church is the main attraction and the surrounding compound is very peaceful. It is worth trying to gain admission to hear the Nuns singing Vespers.

Opening Times:
10.00–11.30 Tuesdays and Thursdays only
Ring the bell

Souvenir Shop: None

Toilets: None

Custodian: The White Nuns of the Russian Orthodox Church.

Telephone: (02) 284371

*　　*　　*

THE KIDRON VALLEY

Also known as the Valley of Jehoshaphat, the literal meaning of which is 'God judges'. In the Book of Joel (3.2) is the prophesy that here all the nations of the world shall be judged, and since the period of the First Temple the slopes of the Kidron Valley have been a favoured site for burials.

There has been a considerable in-fill of the valley over the centuries, but nevertheless the Brook Kidron still flows through it during the winter months.

Much of the water is piped underground, but in places there is an open concrete channel as visible in the orchard immediately to the west of the Church of the Agony. During the summer months it is totally dry.

A little further down the valley can be seen the conical roof of what is generally known as the 'Tomb of Absalom'. This, together with other tombs hewn out of the same rockface, dates from the first century BC. They are among the few surviving artefacts upon which Jesus would undoubtedly have cast his eyes and as such are of particular significance to the Christian.

There is also the moving thought that on Maundy Thursday night Jesus, having been arrested in the Garden of Gethsemane, must have passed this way to his trial and been all too conscious of the fact that on the morrow he himself would lie in a tomb.

The Temple Area

This extensive area encompassing the summit of Mount Moriah is sacred to the three great monotheistic faiths: Jews, Christians and Muslims – half the human race.

Access (see map on page xvi)

The Temple Area with its Western Wall, is situated in the south-east corner of the Old City and comprises a fifth of its area.

1. *On foot:* From within the Jaffa Gate or the Zion Gate walk due east and look out for the signs. From inside the Damascus Gate keep to the left and walk straight ahead for about 700 metres until reaching an underpass which leads to the large piazza in front of the Western Wall. To the right of the Wall a narrow path leads up to a gate giving access to the Temple Area.

2. *By car:* Park outside the Dung Gate in the south wall of the Old City. Once inside the gate walk straight ahead to the security check, and beyond it take the narrow path immediately on the right which leads up to a gate giving access to the Temple Area.

History

There is an ancient tradition that here Abraham prepared to sacrifice his son Isaac in obedience to God.

In 1000 BC King David 'built an altar unto the Lord' having purchased the ground from Araunah, the last of the Jebusite Kings, who had used it as a threshing floor.

King Solomon, David's son, built the First Temple on the site in 950 BC. It became a permanent resting place for the Ark of the Covenant. His Temple was destroyed in 586 BC by the Babylonians when the Jews were taken into exile. Fifty years later they were allowed to return and rebuild to the same plan. Apart from a further interruption of worship during the Maccabean Revolt in 167 BC, the area continued to be the religious centre for the Jews.

Construction of the existing Temple platform, an area of about 35 acres, was begun by Herod the Great in 20 BC and today bears witness to the incredible achievement of his engineers. Upon this platform Herod built the magnificent 'Second Temple' which was still being completed in Our Lord's time.

Here Jesus was Presented as a baby, and here at the age of twelve, his parents found him lingering among the teachers. Later, as an adult, it is recorded that he was tempted by the devil to throw himself down from 'The Pinnacle'.

Jesus often worshipped and taught within its precincts when visiting Jerusalem for one of the major festivals. Shortly before his arrest, he overturned the tables of the money-changers protesting that his Father's house should be a place of prayer and not a den of thieves.

In AD 70 when Jerusalem was sacked by the Roman Emperor Titus, the Temple was totally destroyed and has never been rebuilt. In 135 the Emperor Hadrian reconstructed the City as 'Aelia Capitolina' giving it the layout typical of a Roman town. He virtually ignored the Temple platform and it lay almost derelict for the next five hundred years, although some scholars suggest that a statue or a Temple to Venus was erected on the site.

The Muslims believe that in the middle of the seventh century, it was from the Temple Mount that their Prophet Mohammed ascended into heaven on his winged stallion Al-Burak. For the last thirteen hundred years therefore the area has been sacred to Islam.

Today strict Orthodox Jews are forbidden from entering the area. Because it was the resting place of the Ark of the Covenant the ground is still regarded as too sacred to walk upon. Instead, they worship at the Western Wall which increasingly has become the focal point of Jewish religious life.

Tour

From the approach path there is a good view, on the left, of the Western Wall. The first seven courses of huge stone blocks above the present pavement level are Herodian. In Our Lord's time a deep valley ran beside the wall and eight additional lower courses were also visible. Through the centuries this valley, the Tyropean, has been progressively filled-in with masonry and rubble. Originally two wide bridges spanned the valley so that the Temple could be reached from the Upper City. On the right of the approach path, jutting out from the wall, can clearly be seen the stub of an arch which supported one of them. This is known as 'Robinson's Arch': named after its discoverer the American archaeologist.

Inside the entrance gate and on the right is the Islamic Museum while straight ahead is the Mosque of El-Aqsa. An admission ticket to the Museum and the Mosques can be purchased from the booth in the middle of the open courtyard on the right. The area is strictly controlled by the Muslims and consequently pilgrims should be warned that group readings, prayers and hymns are forbidden. Visitors are also prohibited from sitting on the grass and any unseemly behaviour would mean instant expulsion because the guards are anxious to maintain the sanctity of the site.

It seems likely that somewhere in this southern section of the Temple platform Jesus would have overturned the tables of the money-changers. Beyond the El-Aqsa Mosque, at the far south-eastern corner, there is a sheer drop of about 40 metres from the top of the walls to the bedrock below. This has traditionally become known as 'The Pinnacle' from which Jesus was tempted by the devil to throw himself down and be upheld by the angels. However, access to this point is often forbidden. A good view of 'The Pinnacle' can be gained from the Kidron Valley.

*   *   *

The Mosque of El-Aqsa

Before entering the building visitors must remove their shoes in the Muslim tradition, and for security reasons cameras and hand-baggage are not allowed. Nevertheless a visit is well worthwhile

because the interior is most impressive and the sense of space is truly awesome. There is room for over 4000 Muslims to prostrate themselves on the carpets during their worship which takes place five times a day.

The name means 'the farthest' (from Mecca). Although considerable reconstruction and restoration has been carried out since 1938, the line of the present building dates from the eleventh century and its structure was based on an earlier mosque built in AD 715 by Caliph Al-Wail. During the Crusader period the building was converted for Christian use and became known as the 'Templum Solomonis', headquarters of the Knights Templars. After their defeat in 1187 it was once again used as a mosque. In 1927 serious earthquake damage occurred and more than a third of the structure had to be totally rebuilt. Tragically on August 21st 1969 a visiting Australian deliberately started a fire causing considerable damage to the ancient marble panelling and mosaics at the far end of the building, but the most serious loss was the total destruction of the splendid twelfth century pulpit beautifully inlaid with mother of pearl and ivory.

The roof is supported by 75 columns and pillars which divide the building into a wide nave and six aisles. The circular marble columns are modern and were quarried in Italy, but the massive square pillars on the right date from the eleventh century. The nave and all to the left of the building has been reconstructed since 1938. The 42 clerestory windows containing contemporary coloured glass throw a subdued light on the beautifully decorated ceiling, a gift from King Farouk and the Egyptian Government. The oriental carpets are Turkish, while the green and white prayer rugs were a gift from Saudi-Arabia. The oldest part of the building is the far end where the wall and the mihrab (prayer niche) date from the eighth century. The windows flanking this area contain copies of 12th–14th century stained glass. Notice the modern western-style clock on the left with additional faces indicating sunrise and sunset, and also the variable prayer times throughout the day.

On Fridays the Temple Area is closed all day to tourists when this great mosque, together with the courtyard outside, is filled with thousands of Muslim worshippers.

On leaving the main entrance, walk straight ahead towards the Dome of the Rock and observe, in passing, the ritual cleansing fountain which is in daily use.

The Dome of the Rock

Sometimes called the Mosque of Omar, it is not however a congregational mosque but rather a place for private prayer, contemplation and pilgrimage. This truly magnificent shrine, the earliest surviving Muslim building in existence, was built in AD 692 by Abd-al-Malik and its basic structure has successfully withstood the ravages of time. It was erected over the exposed rock at the summit of Mount Moriah, where according to tradition Abraham prepared to sacrifice his son Isaac, and also in a sacred area where once stood Solomon's Temple, and later the Temple built by Herod the Great which was so familiar to Our Lord. During the Crusader period the building was used as a church, the 'Templum Domini' when for a short time the Christian cross replaced the half crescent.

The perfect geometric proportions and the brilliant blue exterior are particularly striking. Originally the dome was covered in gold and the walls with mosaics. In the sixteenth century the mosaics were replaced by blue turkish tiles and later, at the end of the nineteenth century, a decorative band was added at the top of the outer walls bearing quotations from the Koran. Considerable restoration has taken place in recent years; the gold covering

on the dome has twice been replaced and the wall tiles have been faithfully renewed.

Entrance for visitors is normally through a door in the west face. Again shoes must be removed and there are the usual security arrangements.

The interior at first appears to be rather dark, but the eyes soon adjust to the soft light filtering through the 56 stained glass windows. From the doorway walk towards the centre where, protected by a twelfth century cedar wood screen, can be seen the exposed rock of the top of Mount Moriah. The dome above, decorated with magnificent gold and red stucco, was rebuilt in 1022 but has been partially restored on five separate occasions. The drum supporting it is covered in superb mosaics which follow the original designs. During the Crusader period a Christian altar was placed

upon the rock. The entire area had to be protected by marble because pieces were being chipped away to be used as relics all over Europe.

In the right hand corner of the rock is a tall wooden shrine with gilded grilles and cupola. It is said to contain a hair of the Prophet Mohammed's beard.

Continue around the rock until reaching 16 steps leading down to an ancient cave below. This is a place of great sanctity and there are many fables and legends attached to it in Jewish and Islamic traditions. During the Crusader period the cave was used as a confesssional.

Before leaving the main building notice the splendid mosaics in gold and green at the top of the arcade of outer pillars and arches. Most of the decoration here is original and dates from AD 692. Above it, in gold lettering on a green background, is the founder's inscription running around the building on both sides of the arcade for a total length of 240 metres. It is the oldest arabic script in existence. The Caliph al-Ma'mun in carrying out restoration in 830 erased the name of the founder, Abd-al-Malik, and inserted his own – but he neglected to alter the date!

Once outside the Dome of the Rock, walk to a point on the east of the building to view the little **'Dome of the Chain'**. Some scholars suggest that it was used as a builder's model for the main mosque and was never dismantled. The 17 marble pillars from earlier Byzantine churches are arranged in such a way that they can all be seen simultaneously from any angle. This delightful aedicule is devoid of walls except for a mihrab facing Mecca. It derives its name from an ancient legend that here on the site of David's Place of Judgement a suspended chain was used as a lie detector.

Continue in an easterly direction to descend a wide flight of steps from where there is an attractive view of the Mount of Olives. At the bottom take the path to the left and, on the right of it can be seen the rear of the **Golden Gate**. According to Jewish tradition it is sealed until the Day of Judgement when the righteous will be accepted into the Holy City.

Jesus expels the traders and heals the blind and lame
(Matt 21 .12–17)

Jesus went into the temple and drove out all who were buying and selling in the temple precincts; he upset the tables of the money-changers and the seats of the dealers in pigeons, and said to them, 'Scripture says, "My house shall be called a house of prayer"; but you are making it a bandits' cave.'

In the temple the blind and the crippled came to him, and he healed them. When the chief priests and scribes saw the wonderful things he did, and heard the boys in the temple shouting, 'Hosanna to the Son of David!' they were indignant and asked him, 'Do you hear what they are saying?' Jesus answered, 'I do. Have you never read the text, "You have made children and babes at the breast sound your praise aloud"?' Then he left them and went out of the city to Bethany, where he spent the night. (REB)

'All glory, laud, and honour
to thee, Redeemer, King,
To whom the lips of children
Made sweet hosannas ring.'

For further Gospel references, see page 198

Visitors are discouraged from closely inspecting the structure which is an impressive one dating possibly from the middle of the fourth century. The gate has not been opened since the Crusader period and then only on Palm Sunday and on the Feast of the Exultation of the Cross.

Before leaving the Temple Area, walk along the north side of the compound to notice, on the right, the remaining foundations of Herod's massive **Fortress of Antonia** built directly upon the bedrock. Here was stationed the Roman garrison whose duty it was to maintain public order in the Temple Precincts.

Opening Times:
8.00–11.30 12.30–15.00 7.30–10.00 only during Ramadan
Closed Fridays and Muslim public holidays

Souvenir Shop: None

Toilets: Ask one of the guards for directions

Custodian: The Supreme Muslim Council

Telephone: (02) 283313

Pool of Bethesda

St Anne's Church

Excavations have uncovered a small area of the Pool some ten metres below today's ground level. St John records that here Jesus healed the man who had been paralysed for thirty eight years.

The Crusader Church of St Anne is built over the reputed site of the home of St Joachim and St Anne, the parents of the Virgin Mary.

Access (see map on page xvi)

Approximately sixty metres inside St Stephen's Gate (also known as the Lion Gate) on the right of the street, is the entrance to the compound of the Greek–Catholic Seminary occupied by French White Fathers. There is an inscription to this effect above the doorway. Within the area are located both the Pool of Bethesda and the Church of St Anne.

THE POOL OF BETHESDA

Details

From the entrance door walk straight ahead across the pleasant courtyard past the west facade of St Anne's Church towards the railings which mark the perimeter of the excavations. At first sight the ruins are somewhat bewildering and it is therefore worth studying the archaeological plan close at hand.

The diggings, carried out since 1956, have revealed the remains of a very large fifth century Byzantine Church – the Church of the Paralytic – part of which was built over a small area of the Pool of Bethesda. This was destroyed by the Persians in AD 614 and its masonry fell into the Pool. Today a series of stairways eventually lead down to a level where it is possible to see small pockets of rather stagnant water among the ruins.

In Our Lord's time the Pool was an elongated trapezoid shape approximately 100 metres × 50 metres and over 6 metres deep. It was carved out of the rock as two separate basins. These were surrounded by five colonnades, one on each side and another across the dividing wall. St John refers to them in his Gospel. The Pool was originally built as a reservoir to collect the winter rains which drained into it for use in the Temple during the summer months. The water was believed to have therapeutic qualities and it is interesting to note that the eastern end of the Byzantine Church was built over a pagan Temple to Aesculapius, the Greek God of Healing.

In the twelfth century when the Crusaders built the Church of St Anne, they also erected a small chapel on the remains of the northern nave of the Byzantine Basilica. This can be distinguished very clearly above ground level and affords an excellent example of one church being built upon another.

* * *

THE CHURCH OF ST ANNE

Details

This is one of the finest examples in the Holy Land of a large Crusader Church. From the outside the robust structure gives a fortress-like appearance. Inside, its lines are powerful and rather austere looking very much as they must have done 800 years ago.

From the south aisle 23 steps lead down to the crypt which dates from the fifth century. There is a tradition that the original Byzantine Church was built over a cave which had been part of the home of Joachim and Anne, the parents of the Virgin Mary. The crypt contains two small altars.

The earliest recorded associations with Mary date from the third century when there was an Oratory on the site. Queen Eudoxia, the Byzantine Empress, built the first Church over the Oratory in AD 438. This was destroyed by the Persians at the beginning of the seventh century, but rebuilt soon afterwards. The Crusaders erected the present Church in 1140 and, after they had been driven out half a century later, the Muslims used the buildings as an Islamic theological school, although Christians were still allowed into the crypt. Above the west door outside can be seen an inscription in Arabic from this period.

In 1856 the site was presented to the French by the Turks in appreciation of their help during the Crimean War. Extensive restorations took place before the Church was entrusted to the care of its present occupants the White Fathers.

It is interesting to note that the site was previously offered to Queen Victoria – but this gesture was declined in favour of the Island of Cyprus! Had she accepted the property it is possible that St Anne's might have become the Anglican Cathedral in Jerusalem.

Authors' Comments

The area is a very peaceful haven from the noise of the street outside. St Anne's Church is striking in its simplicity and possesses a fascinating acoustic. Even a small group singing can sound like a large congregation in a great Cathedral.

Opening Times:
Summer: 8.00–1200 14.00–18.00
(Winter: 8.00–12.00 14.00–17.00)
Closed on Sundays

Souvenir Shop: Postcards and a guide book are available

Toilets: Inside the entrance to the compound

Custodian:
The French White Fathers
(A Greek Catholic Community)

Telephone: (02) 283285

The healing of the paralytic (John 5. 2–9a)

Now at the Sheep Gate in Jerusalem there is a pool whose Hebrew name is Bethesda. It has five colonnades and in them lay a great number of sick people, blind, lame, and paralysed. Among them was a man who had been crippled for thirty-eight years.

Jesus saw him lying there, and knowing that he had been ill a long time he asked him, 'Do you want to get well?' 'Sir,' he replied, 'I have no one to put me in the pool when the water is disturbed; while I am getting there, someone else steps into the pool before me.' Jesus answered, 'Stand up, take your bed and walk.' The man recovered instantly; he took up his bed, and began to walk. (REB)

'All your commands I know are true,
your many gifts will make me new,
into my life your power breaks through
Living Lord.'

Via Dolorosa

(The Way of Sorrows)

'The Way of the Cross', the route Jesus took to Calvary, was not defined in its present form until the fifteenth century. There are fourteen Stations of the Cross; nine along The Via Dolorosa and the remainder within the Church of the Holy Sepulchre. Their locations are, in the main, only commemorative; nine are based on the Gospel narratives while the other five are traditional. It is not really practical for large groups to stop for devotions except in the early morning before the shops are opened.

Access

Reference to the map on page xvi will show that there are many approaches, but it is best to enter the Old City from the east through St Stephen's Gate, also known as the 'Lion Gate' because of the four lions in bas-relief on its facade. This gateway and the present walls were built by Suleiman the Magnificent in the sixteenth century. From the gate walk straight ahead for 300 metres.

THE STATIONS OF THE CROSS

(All the Stations are described in detail below; however some pilgrims leave out VIII and IX and proceed straight to number X within the Church of the Holy Sepulchre.)

Station I:
Jesus is Condemned to Death

Located 300 metres from St Stephen's Gate within the courtyard of the Al'Omariyeh College, an Arab school, which now stands over part of the site of the Fortress of Antonia where traditionally Jesus stood trial before Pilate. The Station however is not specifically marked. In order to reach the school, ascend a flight of steps on the left of the road. The premises are not normally open but permission to enter is occasionally given by the gatekeeper. However the Franciscans organise a procession commencing here at 15.00 on Friday afternoons when a heavy wooden cross is carried along the Via Dolorosa. Members of the public are welcome to join them.

In Our Lord's time the Antonia Fortress was an enormous military garrison built by Herod to defend the northern boundary of the City and to maintain order in the Temple Area. Many scholars support the view that Pilate would have stayed in the Fortress whenever he visited Jerusalem from his headquarters at Caesarea beside the Mediterranean. In consequence the traditional Via Dolorosa starts at this point, although some suggest that the Procurator may have stayed in Herod's Palace which was on the west of the City beside the present Jaffa Gate.

Station II:
Jesus takes up The Cross

Like the first Station, the second is not specifically defined. However pilgrims meditate upon its significance in the street a little further along from the steps leading up to the Omariyeh School. Ahead, the arch with the windows above it, is known as 'Ecce Homo' (Behold the Man). It is built on the

site of the Gateway where by tradition Pilate addressed the crowd.

If time allows, there are three important Christian shrines in the immediate vicinity which should be visited. It is widely believed that these are also on part of the site of the Fortress of Antonia. In order to reach them, walk back along the road for a few metres, and enter a doorway on the left just before a smaller arch which spans the street towards the Omariyeh School. The door leads into a courtyard belonging to the Franciscans. Immediately ahead is the entrance to a Roman Catholic theological college, while on the right is:

The Chapel of the Flagellation. This was re-built in 1929 to a design by the Italian architect Antonio Barluzzi. The main features are the ceiling above the altar representing a crown of thorns, and the three stained glass windows. These depict: Jesus scourged at the pillar, Pilate washing his hands, and the triumph of Barabbas.

The Chapel of the Condemnation is on the left of the courtyard. Here behind the altar is a moving portrayal in relief of Jesus leaving the Fortress of Antonia to receive his Cross. Notice the enormous flagstones at the back of the chapel. These are a continuation of the Lithostrotos (pavement) the major part of which can be seen within the adjoining Convent of the Sisters of Zion. Opposite the chapel entrance is a model of Jerusalem in the first century showing how the sites of Calvary and the Tomb were outside the City walls.

The Lithostrotos (the Greek name for Pavement; *Gabbatha* in Aramaic, the spoken language of some of the Jews in Our Lord's time). The entrance is 40 metres further along the street from the courtyard of the Chapels of the Flagellation and Condemnation. At this point turn right into a narrow alley, the door is immediately on the left. Ring the bell for admission. A small entrance fee is payable at the desk and a leaflet will be provided explaining the archaeological discoveries. In the reception area are three information bays and below each lectern will be found some useful explanatory diagrams.

Follow the arrows around the site; the various features are clearly marked. There are many steps to negotiate so the less mobile are advised to turn right at the bottom of the first flight, proceed ahead under an arch, and then turn right again towards the Roman pavement.

The more agile can continue down another flight of steps, almost immediately below the first flight, leading to the Struthion Pool which still holds a large volume of water. This reservoir dates from the Herodian period and its original purpose was to provide water for the Fortress of Antonia and its environs. The vaulted roof here was constructed by Hadrian in AD 135 and it supports a section of the Roman pavement above.

Continue following the arrows around the complex until reaching a level area near the bottom of the first flight of stairs leading down from the entrance foyer. Walk straight ahead and pass over a grille through which can be seen directly below, the waters of the Struthion Pool. A little further along the Roman pavement is reached.

In this area silence is particularly requested because the low ceiling is very resonant. An altar has been erected in the centre for the celebration of Mass.

Notice how the flagstones have gullies cut into them to carry away the rainwater; other sections are striated to prevent horses from slipping, while some of the holes were most probably used to support street lamps.

Proceed to the far end, passing the altar on the left, and notice on the wall a modern mosaic depicting Jesus on the pavement with his Cross.

Now turn back, passing the

altar on the other side, and just beyond on the left is one of the most interesting features of the whole area. Here, etched into a flagstone, can clearly be distinguished the outline of a dice-game played by the Roman soldiers. This was known as the 'King's Game' and occasionally, the soldier who won it was given the robe of the prisoner to be crucified. The game therefore has particular significance in relation to the Gospel story.

Archaeologists have now confirmed that the pavement, as it is seen today, was laid in AD 135 by Hadrian when Jerusalem became a Roman City known as 'Aelia Capitolina'. Although this was a century after the crucifixion, it seems improbable that in the reconstruction, Herod's enormous flagstones would have been totally discarded merely to be substituted by others of similar proportions. It is more likely that many of them would simply have been re-cut and re-laid when the area became a Roman forum. If this assumption is correct, then there are possible grounds for believing that Jesus may have walked on some of these stones.

The exit from the pavement is on the right. Ascend a metal stairway leading to a vestibule from which a revolving steel door gives access to the street. Turn right, walk under the 'Ecce Homo' arch, and then ascend a flight of steps on the right. These lead into a vestibule from where can be seen the interior of the chapel belonging to the Sisters of Zion. The archway behind the altar is Roman. When it was built in AD 135 it formed part of Hadrian's Triumphal Arch the central span of which straddled the street outside.

Return to the Via Dolorosa, walk down the hill for about 100 metres and turn sharp left at the end. Continue for a further 12 metres where, on the left, is:

Station III:
Jesus falls for the first time

Commemorated by a very small chapel, running parallel to the street, above the entrance of which is a stone-relief of Jesus falling with his Cross. Beside the doorway are two ancient pillars. The building was restored in 1948 with donations from Polish soldiers who served in Palestine during the Second World War. Continue along the road for 25 metres and on the left is:

Station IV:
Jesus meets his Mother

Above a doorway the scene is depicted in stone-relief. Here pilgrims are reminded of Mary's grief. The doors lead into a small Armenian Catholic chapel, but it is rarely open to the public. Walk along the road for a further 25 metres and then turn right. On the corner is:

Station V:
Simon of Cyrene is compelled to carry The Cross

The Gospels record how this casual visitor from North Africa became involved in the Passion story. The lintel of a doorway is clearly marked with an inscription, on the left of which is the Roman numeral 'V'. Behind the door is a Franciscan oratory, but again it is not often open to the public. Now start ascending the steps up the hill and in 100 metres on the left is:

Station VI:
St Veronica wipes the sweat from Jesus' face

Reputed to be on the site of the home of St Veronica who, according to tradition, used her veil to wipe the face of Jesus. The imprint of his features remained on the cloth. The veil is said to have been responsible for a number of miracles and since AD 707 has been preserved in St Peter's, Rome.

To identify the Station look for a wooden door with studded metal bands upon it. The centre panel bears the Roman numerals 'VI'. The chapel behind is not open to the public but 10 metres further on, up a flight of steps, the Greek Church of the Holy Face and St Veronica can be

viewed through a metal door. This delightful chapel built in 1882 on the site of a sixth century monastery, was tastefully restored in 1953 by the Italian architect Antonio Barluzzi. It belongs to the Little Sisters of Jesus, a Greek–Catholic Order.

Continue on up the hill for 75 metres. From a position at the end of a very dark archway look directly ahead to identify:

Station VII:
Jesus falls for the second time

On the wall, above a window which is over a doorway, are the Roman numerals 'VII'. The door is often hidden by market stalls and is usually locked. Behind the facade there are two chapels, one above the other, and in the lower is a second century pillar in its original position which was part of the wide colonnaded main street of the Roman city 'Aelia Capitolina'. The thoroughfare, known as the Cardo, ran from the Damascus Gate in the north to the Zion Gate in the south.

It is important to realise that the position of this Station marks the western boundary of Jerusalem in Our Lord's time. According to some scholars, the 'Gate of Judgement' would have been here. From this point onwards therefore Jesus carried his Cross *outside* the City walls on his way to the mound known as 'Golgotha' (Place of the

Skull) upon which crucifixions took place in full view from the walls.

(If pilgrims are leaving out Stations VIII and IX, the following route should be taken to the Church of the Holy Sepulchre. Turn *left* at the top of the hill by Station VII and proceed along the busy main street for 120 metres. Here turn right, then shortly left and right again into a wide thoroughfare. Continue straight ahead for 80 metres and go through a small archway above which are the words 'Holy Sepulchre'.)

Otherwise walk straight across the main thoroughfare into the narrower street, and in only 30 metres look out on the left for:

Station VIII:
Jesus consoles the women of Jerusalem

Of all the Stations this is the most difficult to identify, and it is not even marked with the Roman numerals 'VIII'. Look for a small stone set at eye level among others in a wall. It is distinguished by a cross carved upon it flanked by the Greek letters 'IC XC NIKA' ('Jesus is victorious'). Also cut into the stone is a hole in which a small candle is sometimes placed.

Instructions for reaching the ninth station are somewhat complicated because it is first necessary to retrace one's steps to the main thoroughfare. Here, turn right and walk along the very busy street for 100 metres and, on the right, is a flight of 28 wide steps. Ascend them, turning left at the top, and continue along a passageway for 30

metres and then turn right at the end.

Proceed for 20 metres passing under an archway, turn left at the end and then continue for a further 30 metres until reaching the entrance to the Coptic Patriarchal Cathedral. To the left are three steps leading into the Ethiopian monastery. Here is:

Station IX:
Jesus falls for the third time

The Station is not specifically marked, but pilgrims meditate upon its significance in the vicinity of the ancient Roman column set into the wall.

The remaining five Stations of the Cross are within the Church of the Holy Sepulchre. If the door to the Ethiopian monastery is open, it is possible to take a short cut from this point. The first paragraph below gives instructions for the shorter route. If the door is closed, please read on to the second paragraph.

1. Step into the Ethiopian compound (details of the monastery will be found under 'The Church of the Holy Sepulchre' on page 53). Walk straight ahead and enter the second small door on the right with a low lintel. This leads into the upper chapel belonging to the Abyssinian monks. Walk to the back and descend some steps into the lower chapel. From here a door gives access to the courtyard in front of the main entrance to the Church of the Holy Sepulchre.

2. If the door is not open it will be necessary to return to the main street. Here (at the bottom of the

28 wide steps) turn right and proceed for a further 40 metres to the end. Now turn right, then shortly left and right again into a wide thoroughfare. Continue straight ahead for 80 metres towards a small archway above which are the words 'Holy Sepulchre' leading into the courtyard in front of the Church.

Stations X to XIV are listed here to avoid interruption of the devotional sequence. Except for a brief explanation of the Tomb, no attempt is made in this text to describe the surroundings. A more detailed account can be found under 'The Church of the Holy Sepulchre' on page 46.

From the courtyard in front of the Church of the Holy Sepulchre enter the main door and once inside, turn immediately right to ascend the 19 very steep steps leading to the chapels constructed above the rock of Calvary. The four Stations here are not specifically marked.

Stations X and XI:
Jesus is stripped of his garments
Jesus is nailed to the Cross

The chapel at the top of the stairs belongs to the Roman Catholic Church. Devotions commemorating the Xth and XIth Stations take place here. The two sanctuaries on Calvary are divided by large pillars. Walk between them into the other chapel owned by the Greek Orthodox Church. This is:

Station XII:
Jesus dies on The Cross

The ornate altar here is built directly over the traditional site of the Crucifixion. On either side, through glass panels, can be seen the natural bedrock of Calvary. To the right is:

Station XIII:
Jesus is taken down from The Cross

The small altar placed centrally between the two larger ones also belongs to the Roman Catholic Church. Upon it, protected by glass, is a statue of the Blessed Virgin Mary known as 'Stabat Mater' (Our Lady of Sorrows).

Leave Calvary by the other steps at the rear of the Greek Orthodox chapel, turn left at the bottom and proceed past the Stone of the Anointing above which hang eight lamps. According to tradition it was here that Our Lord's body was prepared for burial. Continue straight ahead to the final Station beneath the Rotunda.

Station XIV:
Jesus is laid in the Tomb

This area of the Church is known as the Anastasis (Resurrection). In the centre is a large aedicule built over the site of the Tomb. It should be remembered that at the beginning of the eleventh century the original tomb was totally destroyed on the orders of the fanatical Egyptian,

Caliph Hakim. The present aedicule marking the sacred place of Our Lord's burial was erected by the Turkish authorities less than two hundred years ago when relations between the East and the West were at a very low ebb. The general impression is not helped by the steel girders which had to be used to shore-up the building following an earthquake in 1927.

Jesus before Pilate. The Way of the Cross (Mark 15. 1–21)

As soon as morning came, the whole Council, chief priests, elders, and scribes, made their plans. They bound Jesus and led him away to hand him over to Pilate. 'Are you the king of the Jews?' Pilate asked him. 'The words are yours,' he replied. And the chief priests brought many charges against him. Pilate questioned him again: 'Have you nothing to say in your defence? You see how many charges they are bringing against you.' But, to Pilate's astonishment, Jesus made no further reply.

At the festival season the governor used to release one prisoner requested by the people. As it happened, a man known as Barabbas was then in custody with the rebels who had committed murder in the rising. When the crowd appeared and began asking for the usual favour, Pilate replied, 'Would you like me to release the king of the Jews?' For he knew it was out of malice that Jesus had been handed over to him. But the chief priests incited the crowd to ask instead for the release of Barabbas. Pilate spoke to them again: 'Then what shall I do with the man you call king of the Jews?' They shouted back, 'Crucify him!' 'Why, what wrong has he done?' Pilate asked; but they shouted all the louder, 'Crucify him!' So Pilate, in his desire to satisfy the mob, released Barabbas to them; and he had Jesus flogged, and then handed him over to be crucified.

The soldiers took him inside the governor's residence, the Praetorium, and called the whole company together. They dressed him in purple and, plaiting a crown of thorns, placed it on his head. Then they began to salute him: 'Hail, king of the Jews!' They beat him about the head with a stick and spat at him, and then knelt and paid homage to him. When they had finished their mockery, they stripped off the purple robe and dressed him in his own clothes.

Then they led him out to crucify him. A man called Simon, from Cyrene, the father of Alexander and Rufus, was passing by on his way in from the country, and they pressed him into service to carry his cross. (REB)

> 'O dearest Lord, thy sacred head
> with thorns was pierced for me:
> O pour thy blessing on my head
> that I may think for thee.'

For further Gospel references, see page 199

The outer chamber is known as the Chapel of the Angel and on a plinth in the centre is reputed to be a piece of the original rolling stone. The site of the tomb itself is marked by an inner chamber lined with marble and constructed in 1810. Inside there is just sufficient room for three people to kneel in devotion. Pilgrims should be warned however that the Greek Orthodox priest on duty will expect a monetary offering. Many find this a distasteful and distracting act within such a very holy place.

Flagellation and Condemnation
Opening Times:
8.00–12.00 14.00–18.00 daily
(Winter: 8.00–12.00 13.00–17.00)
Custodian: The Franciscans
Telephone: 282936

Lithostrotos
Opening Times:
8.30–12.30 14.00–17.00
(Winter closes 16.30)
Closed on Sundays
Toilets: Beyond the Reception Area
Custodian: The French Sisters of Zion
There is an entrance fee
Telephone: (02) 277292

Holy Sepulchre
Opening Times:
4.30–20.00 daily
(Winter: closes 19.00)
Custodian: Multi-denominational
Telephone: (02) 273314
(Franciscans)

Church of the
Holy Sepulchre

This great Basilica encompasses all that remains of the traditional rock of Calvary and the site of Our Lord's tomb. Both are at the very heart of the Christian faith – the scene of man's Redemption, and the place where Jesus overcame the power of death. Of all the holy sites it is undoubtedly the most difficult to come to terms with and in order to appreciate the Church the pilgrim should first have some understanding of its complexity. The archaeological and historical evidence to support the validity of the site is very substantial.

1. The Basilica is not laid out in the traditional western form and at first sight the interior hardly resembles a church at all. The main entrance leads into a dark transept on the south side from which, immediately on the right, steps lead up to two ornate chapels built over the rock of Calvary.

2. Ironically, because of its importance, this central shrine of Christendom has through the centuries suffered from man's attempts alternately at desecration, preservation, and over-zealous adornment. The

present building is the fourth on the site and was erected by the Crusaders in the twelfth century. The original Basilica, built by the Roman Emperor Constantine in AD 335 was almost twice the length.

3. The building is shared by the Armenian, Coptic, Greek Orthodox and Roman Catholic Churches. Although today there is a greater degree of ecumenical tolerance between these branches of Christianity, it is hardly surprising that they jealously guard their ancient rights to hold their own forms of worship within its walls. The very diverse services – and the particular 'territories' owned by the custodians – are strictly governed by regulations known as the 'status quo'. Other Eastern Orthodox Churches within the Holy City are also allowed specific privileges to conduct their worship here.

Furthermore, a vast number of Christian pilgrims from all over the world come to pray in this holy place. To them must be added an even greater number of tourists who also wish to see inside the building. Consequently be prepared for crowds at peak periods.

The most suitable time to visit is very early in the day, and especially from about six o'clock on Sunday morning when this great Basilica – more appropriately known by the Eastern Orthodox Churches as The Church of the Resurrection – can be seen at its best and is alive with so many forms of liturgical worship.

Access (see map on p. xvi)

From the Jaffa Gate: Walk straight ahead into the Old City for 100 metres until reaching the top of David Street, a main Arab trading thoroughfare. Descend the shallow steps for 60 metres and then turn first left under an archway. Continue along this street, Christian Quarter Road, for about 100 metres and look out for the huge stone blocks which now form part of the pavement. These have been moved from their original position but date from the time of Herod the Great. Soon after this turn right into a covered street and walk to the end. Here, by the entrance to a Mosque, turn left and descend some steps which lead into the courtyard in front of the Church of the Holy Sepulchre.

From the Damascus Gate: Pass through the gateway and walk straight ahead for 60 metres keeping to the right. Now take the narrow arched street continuing on the right. Walk along this main thoroughfare to the end (a total distance of 330 metres). At a point where the suq (market) narrows and is traversed by another, turn right into a street open to the skies. Follow the 'S' bend round, and at the junction turn right towards the minaret of a Mosque at the end of a wide street. Proceed straight ahead for 80 metres and go through a small archway above which are the words 'Holy Sepulchre'. This leads into the courtyard in front of the Church.

History and Validity of the Site

For those familiar with the Gospel story and the words of Mrs C. F. Alexander's famous hymn recalling the green hill outside the City walls, it is bewildering to discover that the Church of the Holy Sepulchre is today almost in the centre of the Old City. Scripture clearly records that Christ suffered 'outside the gate' and in a place called Golgotha (the place of the Skull) adjoining which was a garden. It is hardly surprising therefore that some Christians find the Garden Tomb, situated a few hundred metres outside the Damascus Gate, more in keeping with their expectations. Nevertheless the hypothesis is very strong in support of the claim that the ground on which the Church stands was in fact outside the City walls at the time of the Crucifixion.

The Early Archaeological Evidence

1. It is important to appreciate that in Our Lord's lifetime the northern wall of Jerusalem ran roughly from Herod's Palace (where the Citadel now stands) to the Fortress of Antonia. Indeed, one of the purposes of this great stronghold was to defend the City from the north. Golgotha was then *outside* this wall. However, the historian Flavius Josephus records that in the middle of the first century, some time after the Crucifixion, Jerusalem began to spread northwards and a suburb developed. This new area required protection so two other walls were subsequently built.

It was not until AD 135 when the Roman Emperor Hadrian completely redesigned the City, that the northern wall was constructed in its final position. The lower courses of this Roman structure can still be seen below the Damascus Gate. Thus the Church of the Holy Sepulchre is now well within the confines of the Old City and has been for over 1,800 years.

2. In the 1960s the famous British archaeologist, the late Dr Kathleen Kenyon, discovered in a deep excavation south of the church a stone quarry dating from the seventh century BC. This contained only waste material and she found no evidence of any building prior to the second century AD. Consequently she drew the conclusion that the site

39

'remained outside the occupied area, and therefore presumably outside the walls'.

3. Inside the Church of the Holy Sepulchre and within a few metres of the site of Our Lord's Tomb are, hewn out of the bedrock, two complete first century Jewish tombs. This proves that the area was outside the walls in Our Lord's time because burials never took place within the City confines as the ground was thus rendered unclean.

It is probable that there were other tombs in the area and that the rocky mound of Calvary was chosen for crucifixions simply because it could be seen from the walls and acted as a reminder of the consequences of breaking the law.

The Early Historical Evidence

During the four decades after the Resurrection, the followers of Jesus would undoubtedly have known the precise location of Calvary and the Tomb. Many of them had been first hand witnesses to the aftermath of this momentous event – not least among them were Mary Magdalene, Mary the mother of James, Peter and the other disciple who hurried to the Sepulchre on the first Easter morning. Indeed, the Tomb itself most probably remained in Christian hands because it belonged to Joseph of

Aramathea who was a follower of Jesus.

It is important to bear in mind that at this stage these early Christians anticipated that Jesus would return in their own lifetimes. They did not then appreciate the significance of his promise that he would 'be with them always' – in the unseen presence of the Holy Spirit. It was not necessary therefore to physically mark the Tomb for future generations to identify, but it is surely reasonable to assume that the site was venerated by his early followers. They in turn must have passed on very accurate and reliable information as to its exact location. This was the beginning of the 'oral tradition' and it was extremely strong.

In AD 70 the Roman Emperor Titus sacked the City. Herod's magnificent Temple, the centre of Jewish worship and culture, was totally destroyed together with all other buildings of significance. Indeed Jesus himself predicted that 'not one stone would be left upon another'. However it seems most likely that Calvary and the Tomb would have escaped the attention of Titus's troops being already waste ground, an 'unclean' burial place, with no buildings erected upon it.

There then followed a very sad period in Jerusalem's

history when the city lay in ruins, rather like some of those in Europe after the Second World War. However, domestic life gradually began to return to some degree of normality as the inhabitants had not been banished, although many of the Jewish leaders were slain. Thus the seeds of the early Church were able to survive.

Between Pentecost and the destruction of Jerusalem, Christianity spread rapidly throughout the whole of the Eastern Mediterranean due to the activities of St Paul. Antioch became the missionary centre of the Gentile Church, but Jerusalem remained at its heart and James, a brother of Our Lord, became the first Bishop.

In AD 135, sixty-five years after the sacking of the City by Titus, the Jews were finally banished by Hadrian who totally rebuilt Jerusalem in the form of a typical Roman colonial town renamed 'Aelia Capitolina'. He constructed a large podium over the entire area of Calvary and the Tomb upon which were erected in honour of the Roman gods a statue of Jupiter and a Temple to Venus. St Jerome suggests that Hadrian did this in order to obscure the sites and prevent the Christians from venerating them. Whether this is true or not the fact remains that his action marked their position for future generations to uncover.

Although Hadrian had banished the Jews, the Gentile Church of Graeco-Roman origin nevertheless continued. There is an extant record of all the Graeco-Roman Bishops and Eusebius, who was Bishop of Caesarea from AD 313, mentions that the Gentile Church in Jerusalem flourished.

Fourth Century Developments

Early in the fourth century the Roman Emperor Constantine was converted to Christianity by his mother St Helena. Macarius, the Bishop of Jerusalem at that time, assured him that Calvary and the Tomb were to be found beneath the Temple to Venus and the statue of Jupiter. Constantine expressed a desire to 'make that most blessed spot, the place of the Resurrection, visible to all and given over to veneration'.

Consequently in AD 325 work started on demolishing the Temple and removing the podium. The whole area when cleared revealed the small mound of Calvary, while a little to the west rose the rockface containing the Sepulchre. In a letter which Constantine wrote to Bishop Macarius he said: 'No words can express how good the Saviour has been to us . . . that the monument of his Holy Passion, hidden for so many years, has now at last been restored to the faithful and set free by the defeat of

41

our common enemy, it is indeed a miracle. My great wish is, after freeing the site of impious idols, to adorn it with splendid buildings'.

In order to construct his magnificent basilica encompassing these two holy sites the ground had to be levelled, and to fit into the architectural plan the rock surrounding the Tomb was cut away vertically. Calvary also received similar treatment (*see diagrams opposite*). Eusebius wrote: 'Is it not astonishing to see the rock standing isolated, in the midst of a level space, with a cave inside it'.

A large Rotunda was constructed to encircle the Tomb with an open colonnaded courtyard to the east of it. In the south-east corner of this cloister stood the tall block of Calvary, surrounded by a metal grille and with a cross erected on the top. A depiction of this can be seen today in a contemporary fourth century mosaic in the Church of Santa Pudenziana in Rome. Immediately to the east of the colonnaded cloister was built a large basilica known as the Martyrium, dedicated to the martyrdom of the Saviour. Access was from the Cardo, the main Roman street of Jerusalem.

The remains of this entrance are still visible today in the Hospice of the Russian

Excavations, in the cellars of the nearby Coptic Convent, and also in the basement of Zelatino's Cafe at the foot of the steps which lead up to the Ethiopian Monastery from the suq. The extent of the Church is clearly visible in the famous sixth century Madaba mosaic map. Reference to the diagram opposite will explain the probable layout.

The Basilica was consecrated on the 14th September 335 in the presence of 300 Bishops. Thus for over sixteen and a half centuries the Church has been a focus of Christian pilgrimage.

A brief history of the four churches built on the site

1. *Constantine's* Basilica remained in continuous use for nearly three hundred years until AD 614 when it was destroyed by the Persian invaders. However, only a few years passed before they in turn were defeated by the Roman Emperor Heraclius. He gave instructions that the Christian places of worship should be rebuilt.

2. *Modestus*, the Bishop of Jerusalem at that time, set about reconstructing the Church, although on completion his Basilica lacked much of its former grandeur. In 637 the City was overrun by the Muslims, but their leader, the Caliph Omar, spared the building and

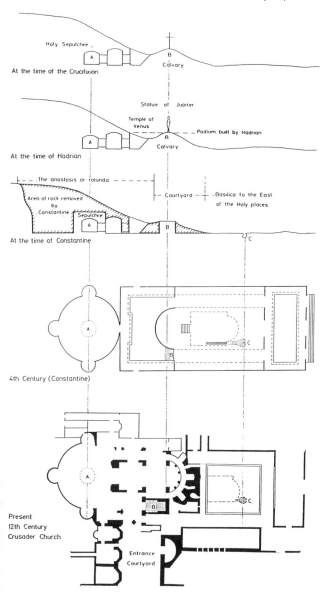

Holy Sepulchre

A

B
Calvary

At the time of the Crucifixion

Statue of Jupiter

Temple of Venus

Podium built by Hadrian

A

B
Calvary

At the time of Hadrian

The anastasis or rotunda

Area of rock removed by Constantine

Sepulchre

A

Courtyard

Basilica to the East of the Holy places

B

C

At the time of Constantine

A

B

C

4th Century (Constantine)

A

B

C

Present 12th Century Crusader Church

Entrance Courtyard

43

allowed the Christians to continue to worship there. It should be borne in mind that Jesus is recognised as a Prophet in the Islamic faith.

Worship continued for nearly four hundred years until AD 1009 when the fanatical Egyptian, Caliph Hakim, began persecuting the Christians. He gave orders that all the churches in the land should be destroyed – and especially the Church of the Holy Sepulchre. There is an interesting account by an observer of how at first the rock of the Tomb seemed almost impenetrable to the workmen's tools. However they persevered and eventually the damage was catastrophic. The Tomb itself was hacked to pieces so that virtually nothing remained. The Basilica then lay in ruins for almost four decades.

3. *Monomachus*, the Roman Emperor, in exchange it is said for 5,000 Muslim prisoners, was given permission to rebuild on the site in 1048. His Basilica was on a scale even less lavish than that of Modestus, but worship resumed and the building continued to be used for fifty years.

4. *The Crusaders* finally captured the City on the 15th July 1099 and immediately set about the total restoration of the Church. The architecture was that of the western tradition and the finest

craftsmen were employed from all over Europe. For the first time the rock of Calvary and the site of the Tomb were enclosed under one roof and a chapel was built over Calvary. A simple aedicule was constructed over the site of the Tomb, and the Rotunda surrounding it was embellished with magnificent carvings. The small surviving crypt from Constantine's Martyrium was dedicated to St Helena as there was a tradition that, in an ancient cistern below it, she had discovered the True Cross and the Instruments of the Passion.

On the 15th July 1149 a great service was held in thanksgiving for the complete restoration. The church must have been one of the finest in the world.

Upon the defeat of the Crusaders, the Augustinian monks became responsible for the building and their monastery was constructed above the Chapel of St Helena. This was destroyed during the Middle Ages, but the remains of the roof arches are still visible encircling the monastery of the Ethiopians who now occupy the site.

In 1808 a fire seriously damaged the Rotunda. At this time, when relations between the East and the West were at a particularly low ebb on account of the Napoleonic Wars, Palestine was ruled by the Turks. Consequently, it was left to the Christians in the East to carry out the restoration. They made a deplorable job of it. The tombs of the Crusader Kings of Jerusalem were removed, the rich stone decorations destroyed, the ambulatory around the Rotunda closed, many windows filled-in, and the stone walls were covered with plaster. The building took on a very dark and dismal appearance. Sadly too, in 1810 the simple Crusader aedicule over the site of the Tomb was replaced by the present somewhat ugly alabaster shrine.

To aggravate the situation further, in 1927 there was a serious earthquake and the whole building had to be temporarily shored-up by British engineers for fear of total collapse. Most of the unsightly girders have now been removed but some can still be seen around the aedicule and also above a flight of steps leading down to the courtyard in front of the church.

Since 1950 there has been a more favourable ecumenical climate, and a team of three architects representing the Armenian, Greek Orthodox, and Roman Catholic Churches has been appointed for the express purpose of trying to restore the building to some degree of its original splendour. The task, not surprisingly, is taking a very

long time because their proposals have to be agreed by Christians from totally different cultural backgrounds. Nevertheless, considerable progress is being made and each year there is some significant improvement.

Tour (Please refer to numbered plan on the next page)

The facade of the Church is in typical Crusader style. Notice the twelfth century decoration around the window and door arches. The original carved lintels were removed to the Rockefeller Museum for safekeeping following the 1927 earthquake. The right-hand doorway has been blocked since the sixteenth century. In the pavement in front of this, under some wooden slats, is the tomb of the English Knight, Philip d'Aubigny, tutor to Henry III. In 1810 when all the other Crusader tombs were desecrated it escaped destruction because it was hidden by the doorkeeper's bench.

Since the defeat of the Crusaders in 1187 the responsibility for locking and unlocking the door of this most important shrine in Christendom has remained with the Muslims. For the past four hundred years the duty has been shared by the same two families who have zealously guarded their

45

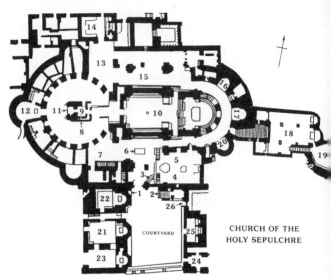

CHURCH OF THE
HOLY SEPULCHRE

privilege. One has the custody of the key, while the other performs the actual opening. The Christians still have to pay them a fee for doing so!

The massive bell tower on the left (1) has been standing since the twelfth century although the top storey had to be dismantled in 1549 following an earthquake. The steps on the right (2) originally led up into a porchway giving access to the chapels above Calvary. Since the Middle Ages the entrance has been blocked, and today the area beneath the cupola is known as the Chapel of the Franks. Below this is a small Greek oratory dedicated to St Mary of Egypt.

Enter the Church, and allow time to adjust from the bright light outside. Almost behind the front doors turn immediately right to ascend 19 very steep steps (3) which lead up to the two chapels above Calvary. The first belongs to the Roman Catholics and commemorates the Nailing to the Cross (4). In the ceiling in front of the altar, darker than its surround, is portrayed a figure of Christ – the only remaining Crusader mosaic in the entire building. The chapel was restored in 1937, however the Florentine altar dates from 1588. The Xth and XIth Stations of the Cross are venerated here. Through the grille on the right can be seen the Chapel of the Franks, the original approach to the shrine.

On the left, beyond the central pillar, is the extremely ornate Greek Orthodox Chapel of Calvary (5). The altar is sited directly over the place where, it is believed, the Cross stood. The glass panels on either side reveal the natural rock below. Also visible is a rent in the rock which geologists agree was occasioned by an earthquake. It could well have been the one which occurred at the Crucifixion. The XIIth Station of the Cross is venerated here.

Between the two chapels is another Roman Catholic altar dedicated to 'Stabat Mater' (Our Lady of Sorrows). This is the XIIIth Station of the

---

The Crucifixion (Mark 15. 22–39)

They brought Jesus to the place called Golgotha, which means 'Place of a Skull', and they offered him drugged wine, but he did not take it. Then they fastened him to the cross. They shared out his clothes, casting lots to decide what each should have. It was nine in the morning when they crucified him; and the inscription giving the charge against him read, 'The King of the Jews'. Two robbers were crucified with him, one on his right and the other on his left.

The passers-by wagged their heads and jeered at him . . . 'So you are the man who was to pull down the temple, and rebuild it in three days! Save yourself and come down from the cross.' The chief priests and scribes joined in, jesting with one another: 'He saved others,' they said, 'but he cannot save himself. Let the Messiah, the king of Israel, come down now from the cross. If we see that, we shall believe.' Even those who were crucified with him taunted him.

At midday a darkness fell over the whole land, which lasted till three in the afternoon; and at three Jesus cried aloud, 'Eloi, Eloi, lema Sabachthani?' which means, 'My God, my God, why have you forsaken me?' Hearing this, some of the bystanders said, 'Listen! He is calling Elijah.' Someone ran and soaked a sponge in sour wine and held it to his lips on the end of a stick. 'Let us see', he said, 'if Elijah will come to take him down.' Then Jesus gave a loud cry and died; and the curtain of the temple was torn in two from top to bottom. When the centurion who was standing opposite him saw how he died, he said, 'This man must have been a son of God.' (REB)

'O dearest Lord, thy sacred heart
with spear was pierced for me;
O pour thy spirit on my heart
that I may speak for thee.'

For further Gospel references, see page 197

Cross and commemorates the place where Mary received the body of her Son. The statue above it, enclosed in a glass case, was a gift from Queen Maria I of Portugal in 1778.

Tour continued

Descend the steep steps at the back of the Chapel of Calvary and at the bottom turn left. Ahead, directly opposite the main entrance, flanked by candlesticks and beneath a row of eight hanging lamps can be seen the Stone of the Anointing (6). It belongs jointly to the Armenians, Greeks, and Roman Catholics and commemorates the place where, according to tradition, the body of Our Lord was prepared for burial. The polished red stone dates from the time of the Turkish restoration in 1810. This is the XIVth Station of the Cross.

Continue in the same direction towards four pillars surmounted by a marble canopy which marks the place from where the three Marys are said to have viewed the Crucifixion (7). This area belongs exclusively to the Armenians. Their sacristy is on the left while the stairs lead up to a small oratory.

From the position where the three Marys stood the pilgrim today has his first glimpse of the shrine built over the site of the Tomb (8). This is perhaps appropriate because on seeing it many also experience a sense of bewilderment, incredulity and disbelief. The present aedicule, less than two hundred years old and still encased in steel girders after the 1927 earthquake, is hardly edifying to Christians from the West.

The lofty circular stone structure encompassing this whole area is known as the Rotunda or Anastasis (Resurrection) and was built upon foundations laid over sixteen-hundred years ago (*see diagram on page 43*). Originally the pillars were covered in marble and the cupola glittered with gold mosaics. The interior of the Muslim Dome of the Rock in the Temple Area affords an idea of how splendid it might have looked.

Now proceed to the front of the shrine. Above the doorway are numerous hanging lamps and the entrance is flanked by enormous candlesticks belonging to the Armenians, Greeks and Roman Catholics. The inside is divided into two chambers. The first is the Chapel of the Angel (9) where in the centre is a pilaster which contains, according to tradition, a piece of the original Sepulchre. Some claim that it is part of the rolling stone. A low doorway leads into the second chamber resembling a tomb. It is lined in marble and hung with more lamps and holy pictures.

There is just room for three people to kneel in prayer. A marble slab dating from the sixteenth century represents the place where, it is believed, the body of Jesus lay.

Pilgrims should be warned that during peak periods there is a Greek priest on duty in the chamber who expects a monetary offering. Many find this a particularly distasteful and distracting act within such a very holy place.

The Resurrection (John 20. 1–18)

Early on the first day of the week, while it was still dark, Mary of Magdala came to the tomb. She saw that the stone had been moved away from the entrance, and ran to Simon Peter and the other disciple, the one whom Jesus loved. 'They have taken the Lord out of the tomb,' she said, 'and we do not know where they have laid him.'

So Peter and the other disciple set out and made their way to the tomb. They ran together, but the other disciple ran faster than Peter and reached the tomb first. He peered in and saw the linen wrappings lying there, but he did not enter. Then Simon Peter caught up with him and went into the tomb. He saw the linen wrappings lying there, and the napkin which had been round his head, not with the wrappings but rolled up in a place by itself. Then the disciple who had reached the tomb first also went in, and he saw and believed; until then they had not understood the scriptures, which showed that he must rise from the dead.

So the disciples went home again; but Mary stood outside the tomb weeping. And as she wept, she peered into the tomb, and saw two angels in white sitting there, one at the head, and one at the feet, where the body of Jesus had lain. They asked her, 'Why are you weeping?' She answered, 'They have taken my Lord away, and I do not know where they have laid him.' With these words she turned round and saw Jesus standing there, but she did not recognise him. Jesus asked her, 'Why are you weeping? Who are you looking for?' Thinking it was the gardener, she said, 'If it is you, sir, who removed him, tell me where you have laid him, and I will take him away.' Jesus said, 'Mary!' She turned and said to him, 'Rabbuni!' (which is Hebrew for 'Teacher'). 'Do not cling to me,' said Jesus, 'for I have not yet ascended to the Father. But go to my brothers, and tell them that I am ascending to my Father and your Father, to my God and your God.' Mary of Magdala went to tell the disciples. 'I have seen the Lord!' she said, and gave them his message. (REB)

'Jesus lives! our hearts know well
Nought from us his love shall sever;
Life, nor death, nor powers of hell
Tear us from his keeping ever. Alleluya!'

For further Gospel references, see page 197

Tour continued

Opposite the entrance to the Tomb is the Greek Orthodox Cathedral known as the Katholikon (10). Originally this was the choir of the Crusader church. A great deal of restoration has taken place in recent years and the lofty vaulted ceiling is reminiscent of those in many European Cathedrals. Notice the large screen, the Iconostasis, a feature of the Eastern Orthodox churches, which partially hides the altar from view. From the ceiling hangs an impressive modern chandelier while on the polished marble floor stands the 'omphalos' (navel). To the Greeks this symbolises the centre of the world.

Now walk to a position directly behind the Tomb where the Coptic Church have erected a small chapel (11). Under the altar is displayed a portion of rock which they claim to be part of the original Sepulchre.

Directly opposite this little chapel, walk between two of the pillars supporting the Rotunda into an extremely dilapidated room, the Chapel of the Syrian-Jacobites (12). On Sundays and Feast Days it is furnished and the tiered altar dressed for the celebration of Mass. Notice the curved wall at the back which was part of one of the three apsed-chapels of the original Constantinian Church.

Immediately on the left is the low entrance to a complete first century Jewish tomb. This is extremely important because it proves that the site was outside the City walls at the time of the Crucifixion. (See 'Early Archaeological Evidence' 3. on page 40.)

Return to the Rotunda, and turning left passing the Chapel of the Copts and the Tomb, walk between the pillars of the Rotunda on the left into an area which is exclusively owned by the Roman Catholics (13). Opposite the fine modern organ is an altar dedicated to St Mary Magdalene commemorating the place where Jesus appeared to her on the first Easter morning. To the left of the altar is the Franciscans' private sacristy.

At the far end of this area double-doors lead into the Chapel of the Apparition (14). There is an ancient tradition that Jesus appeared to his mother after his Resurrection, although the event is not recorded in the Gospels. The Franciscans have tastefully restored the chapel and here the Blessed Sacrament is reserved. Inside, the scenes of the Passion are movingly depicted in wrought-iron along the wall. It is a most suitable place for meditation.

On leaving the chapel, pass the altar dedicated to St Mary Magdalene and turn left. Walk along a rather dark aisle known as the Arches of the Virgin containing pillars and other remains from earlier Basilicas (15). Towards the end divert to the left to see a small Greek chapel called the 'Prison of Christ'. The reason for the name is unclear.

Return to the aisle and ahead, at the end, are three other chapels constructed around an ambulatory. The first belongs to the Greeks and is dedicated to St Longinus (16), the Roman Soldier whose spear pierced Our Lord's side, while next to it is another belonging to the Armenians commemorating the Division of the Raiment (17).

Now begin descending, on the left, the 29 steps to the Armenian Chapel of St Helena (18) and notice on the walls hundreds of crosses inscribed by pilgrims. The chapel was the crypt of Constantine's Basilica and is therefore the oldest complete part of the entire building. Notice the dome in the ceiling which outside is seen to be at ground level in the courtyard of the Ethiopian monastery. Since 1950 a major restoration of the chapel has taken place and the walls and floor have been decorated with scenes from Armenian history.

Important archaeological excavations were begun in the 1970s when a most interesting cavernous area was discovered below a storeroom directly behind the main altar. If there is a priest on duty, it is worth seeking his permission to view the excavations which are reached by way of a wrought iron door on the left of the sanctuary. This gives access to part of the seventh century BC quarry mentioned earlier (page 39); remnants of the foundations of the podium constructed by Hadrian in AD 135 upon which he erected his pagan temple; and also some of the foundations of the original Basilica built by Constantine in AD 330. In the centre of the excavated cavern is an altar dedicated to St Vartan and the Armenian Martyrs, but of particular interest on a stone block to the right is a drawing of a fishing boat – a symbol of Christian pilgrimage – claimed to be over 1,600 years old.

Return to the main Armenian chapel and descend the 22 stairs on the right of the altar to the Franciscan Chapel of the Finding of the Cross which has been built within part of the ancient quarry (19). Here, according to tradition, St Helena discovered The True Cross and the Instruments of the Passion. The chapel is a quiet place away from the crowds and affords another opportunity for meditation.

Now return to the main body of the church ascending all the steps and turn left at the top. Almost immediately is the third of the chapels built around the ambulatory (20). This belongs to the Greeks and commemorates the Mocking of Our Lord by the crowd. Continue on, and in about 10 metres notice on the left a glass screen which slightly protrudes into the aisle. Through it can be seen the natural rock of Calvary. Now, almost immediately, turn left into a small area which is directly under the Greek Orthodox Chapel of Calvary where the rock can be seen again and is floodlit behind protective glass. The fissure in the middle is a continuation of the one in the chapel above.

This small place is designated in some guide books as the 'Chapel of Adam'. The Eastern Orthodox Churches perpetuate a somewhat dubious, but nevertheless symbolic, legend that in a cave below the rock of Calvary Adam was buried and the blood of Jesus fell upon the first guilty head. Consequently in many Greek depictions of the Crucifixion a skull appears at the foot of the Cross. St Paul puts it more positively in his First Letter to the Corinthians (1.22): 'For as in Adam all die, so in Christ shall all be made alive'.

A fitting thought with which to conclude a somewhat overwhelming tour of the Church of the Holy Sepulchre.

Opening Times:
4.30–20.00 daily. (Winter: closes 19.00)

Souvenir Shop: None

Toilets: None

Custodians: The Armenian, Greek, and Roman Catholic Churches

Telephone: Franciscans: (02) 273314

There are a number of other chapels, monasteries and convents directly linked to the Church which the pilgrim may possibly gain permission to enter. If time permits a plan of the whole area is obtainable from the Christian Information Centre opposite the moated entrance to the Citadel near the Jaffa Gate (not to be confused with the Tourist Information Office just inside the gate). Five of these places are briefly mentioned below:

1. Three *Greek Orthodox chapels* on the west of the courtyard. It seems likely that the baptistry of the original fourth century Constantinian Basilica would have stood in this area. Archaeological excavation has not been possible, but the middle chapel is dedicated to St John (21) and there is a very ancient baptistry within it. The chapel, directly under the Crusader belfry is in memory of the 'Forty Martyrs', soldiers of the Twelfth Legion who were frozen to death in Armenia in AD 320 rather than renounce their Christian

faith (22). The third chapel at the other end is dedicated to St James (23). This is used by the Greek Orthodox Community as their Parish Church.

2. On the east of the courtyard the door furthest from the Basilica leads into the **Greek Orthodox Convent of St Abraham** (24). Since the end of the last century it has been possible for Anglican groups to seek prior permission from the Greek Patriarch to celebrate a Eucharist in their little chapel very close to Calvary. Application should be made through the Dean of St George's Cathedral.

3. The central arched doorway, on this side of the courtyard, with the modern green and gold doors gives access to the ornately decorated **Armenian Chapel of St John** (25).

4. The door nearest to the Basilica leads into a chapel owned by the Copts but used by the Ethiopian monks (26). Inside, on the left, a stairway ascends to their upper chapel. A passageway to the left of the altar gives access to the courtyard of the **Ethiopian Monastery**. This is directly above the Armenian Chapel of St Helena, the cupola of which is clearly visible at ground level in the centre of the courtyard.

The monastery is a fascinating complex and the pilgrim might be forgiven for thinking that he was in Africa because the dark-skinned monks and nuns live in very simple whitewashed dwellings. From a position beside the far wall of the courtyard there is a good view of the large apse of the Greek Orthodox Katholikon. Notice also on the left the remains of roof-arches from the earlier mediaeval Augustinian Monastery.

5. The Hospice of the Russian Excavations. On leaving the courtyard in front of the Church of the Holy Sepulchre, turn left through the small archway and continue to the end of the street. The Hospice is on the left. Ring the bell, an admission fee is charged. Here excavations carried out in 1883 have revealed part of the podium constructed by Hadrian, and also one of the three entrances to Constantine's Basilica.

The Garden Tomb

This complete tomb which almost certainly existed at the time of Christ is approached through a lovingly-tended garden. It is a most helpful visual aid to the events of the first Easter.

Access

The site lies to the right of the Nablus Road, 250 metres due north of the Damascus Gate.

Sometimes known as 'Gordon's Calvary' because in 1883 General Charles Gordon of Khartoum became convinced that here he had found the true site of Calvary and The Tomb. The nearby rock-face resembled Golgotha (the Place of a Skull) and the site lay outside the City walls, thus conforming to the description in the four Gospels.

The tomb is one of a number of ancient sepulchres in the area, but sadly for many pilgrims there is no historical or archaeological evidence to support the validity of the site. However it undoubtedly appeals to the imagination and is generally considered to be aesthetically more pleasing than the Church of the Holy Sepulchre.

Authors' Comments

A peaceful haven from the busy streets outside which is well worth a visit. Many pilgrims find the atmosphere here more conducive to meditation than the Church of the Holy Sepulchre.

Opening Times:
8.30–12.00 14.00–17.30
Closed on Sundays except for a service at 9.00

Souvenir Shop: At the main entrance. Very well stocked with cards and books.

Toilets: Follow the signs from the shop

Custodians: The Garden Tomb Association

Telephone: (02) 272745

The Citadel

The Tower of David

The fortress today is mainly medieval and the line of the present walls dates from the Crusaders in the twelfth century. Constructed partly on the remains of King Herod's Palace, the lower courses of Herodian dressed stone in the massive north-eastern tower date from the time of Christ. The buildings contain an imaginative museum tracing the history of Jerusalem over a period of three thousand years. An excellent open air 'Son et Lumiere' is also presented in English on some summer evenings.

The Citadel is often referred to as 'The Tower of David' but no connection with that King has ever been established. It was the Byzantines who incorrectly identified the area as the site of his palace – and the name has been handed on through the centuries.

Access

Situated in the west of the Old City adjacent to the Jaffa Gate (see map on page xvi). The main entrance is located on the eastern side of the compound and is approached via a flight of steps. There is an admission charge.

History

The earliest settlements on the site date from the seventh century BC. During the reign of the Hasmonean King, John Hyrcanus (134–104 BC), a defensive city wall was built part of which archaeologists have now uncovered running from north to south through the centre of the compound. King Herod erected his royal palace here on a grand scale. It extended much further south, almost as far as the present city walls and included a large garden. He built three towers and dedicated them to his brother Phasael, his wife Mariamne, and his friend Hippicus but the position of two of these has yet to be discovered. Some scholars are of the opinion that Pontius Pilate would have stayed in Herod's royal palace when he came up to Jerusalem at the time of the major festivals, in preference to residing in the Fortress of Antonia (see page 29). If this is true, then somewhere within the vicinity Jesus would have stood trial before Pilate and been scourged. In AD 66 the palace was burnt down during a Jewish revolt. These uprisings led to the Roman General Titus sacking the City in AD 70. The Tenth Legion then used the area for the next two hundred years as a barracks.

In the twelfth century the Crusader King Baldwin II utilised the site as his palace and constructed new buildings to the west beyond the old defensive city wall. The Citadel was further adapted and fortified by the Marmelukes at the beginning of the fourteenth century and two hundreds years later by Suleiman the Magnificent. He also rebuilt most of the present walls surrounding the Old City. In 1917 General Allenby proclaimed the British liberation of Jerusalem from Turkish rule from the steps in front of the entrance gateway.

Following the Six Day War in 1967 the Citadel was converted into an attractive museum.

Details

All the features are clearly marked, but be sure to climb to the top of the north-eastern tower (with its Herodian lower courses) from which there are fine views across the Old City to the Mount of Olives. It is now known as 'David's Tower' and there is an exhibition room on the first floor. The main Museum comprises three separate areas each covering a specific period of Jerusalem's history. Allow at least two hours to view the exhibits.

Opening Times:
Sunday to Thursday: 9.00–17.00
(Winter: 10.00–16.00)
Friday, Saturday and holiday eves: 9.00–14.00

Souvenir Shop: More than one outlet.

Toilets: Available and well signposted

Custodian: The Municipality of Jerusalem

Telephone: (02) 274111

Son-et-Lumiere: During the summer months performances in English are at 21.30 on Mondays and Wednesdays and 22.30 on Saturdays. Warm clothing is recommended.

The Cathedral of St James

This Armenian Cathedral is undoubtedly one of the more important Christian places in Jerusalem. Its most significant relic is thought to be the head of St James the Great who was executed in AD 44. The Cathedral is also reputed to be the burial place of St James the Less, and is the seat of the Armenian Patriarch.

Access

Admission times are very restricted; see details at end of chapter. Enter the Old City by the Jaffa Gate, follow the road round the high walls of the Citadal passing the bridge leading into the main entrance. Continue for about 150 metres, ahead is a narrow arched covered passageway. Proceed through with caution because there is no pavement and hardly room for both cars and pedestrians. At the end, on the left, is the arched entrance to the Cathedral.

The Armenians

The Armenians were the first people to adopt Christianity as their official state religion in AD 287. The present community in Jerusalem have deep roots in the City and it is interesting to note that from the Crusader period until the end of the Turkish rule in 1918 their Patriarch was considered to be the most senior Christian dignitary in the Holy Land.

The modern Region of Armenia lies south of the Caucasus Mountains and between the Black Sea and the Caspian Sea. Towards the end of the last century there was considerable unrest which resulted in mass genocide carried out by Turkish troops in 1909 and 1915 when it is said that nearly two million people lost their lives.

Today there are about two and a half million Armenians worldwide but many have migrated throughout the Middle East and to the United States. At the beginning of the century some families not surprisingly joined their fellow countrymen in Jerusalem. In more recent times there has been a movement away from Israel, and it is said that the population of the Armenian Quarter has decreased from many thousands to a few hundred. Nevertheless the Armenian Church continues to have considerable influence amongst the Christian communities. It has sole jurisdiction over part of the Church of the Nativity in Bethlehem and also over the

Chapel of St Helena in the crypt of the Church of the Holy Sepulchre.

Tour

The entrance to the Cathedral from the street is through a tall archway which immediately leads into a vestibule. The doorkeeper's office in on the left. Walk diagonally across to the right where an archway leads into a small courtyard. Here some of the inscriptions on the wall date from the twelfth century and include examples of the so-called Jerusalem Cross which originated in Armenia in the 9/10th century. It was later adopted by the Crusaders and the Franciscans. Notice the finely decorated wrought iron screen leading into the ceremonial entrance to the Cathedral.

Ascend the steps on the right and straight ahead are clappers, one in wood and the other in metal. These are still struck with a hammer to summon the faithful to worship – an alternative to bells whose ringing was forbidden at some periods in the past. Notice above the Cathedral's main entrance a painting depicting Christ seated in glory surrounded by the Virgin and other holy men and women. In front of the doorway hangs a heavy leather curtain which effectively acts as a sound barrier.

The interior has many moods; on a sunny day, and particularly during worship when many of the hanging lamps are alight, there is a sense of colour and life; whilst on a cloudy day and when there is no worship, it can in contrast seem extremely dark. The Cathedral is dedicated to St James (the son of Zebedee and brother of St John the Apostle) whom it is said was executed on this site by Herod Agrippa I, grandson of Herod the Great, circa AD 44. (Acts 12. 1–2). It is also dedicated to St James the Less. Some scholars believe that this Apostle was Our Lord's brother who became the first Bishop of Jerusalem.

The walls are partially covered in blue 18th century Turkish tiles and many ornate lamps are suspended from the ceiling. The main altar, and the chapel to the right of it, are dedicated to the Virgin Mary, while the chapel on the left is dedicated to St John the Baptist. Notice the Patriarchal throne of St James the Less adjacent to the large north-east pillar. It was made in 1656 and is used only on ceremonial occasions. Beside it, on the east side of the pillar is a low iron grille enclosing the reputed burial place of the Saint.

Turning to the north wall of the nave; the first small chapel on the left is dedicated to St Macarius, Bishop of Jerusalem at the time of Constantine, while next to it is the vestible of the second slightly larger chapel dedicated to St James the Great. This is the most important shrine in the Cathedral and is reputedly built over the site where the Saint was beheaded. It is said to contain his skull. There is an ancient tradition that the body was taken to Santiago de Compostella in Spain. Notice the extremely fine 18th century decoration on the doors inlaid with tortoiseshell and mother-of-pearl.

Other chapels in the Cathedral are not normally open to the public, but it is worth noting that the doorway beyond the shrine of St James gives access to a complex of chapels including that of the Apostles and altars dedicated to St Minas and St Sargis. Also through the same archway is the entrance to the Church of St Stephen now used as a sacristy. Here too is the baptistery of the Cathedral. Altars within this area are dedicated to St Stephen himself; St Cyril, Bishop of Jerusalem in the fourth century; and St Gregory the Illuminator. This is the oldest part of the building some of which may date from the fifth century.

The present structure of the Cathedral dates mainly from the twelfth century and its original entrance was through the door in the south wall. The exterior of this doorway is in typical Crusader style, and originally it was approached from the south via an arched portico. This was filled in during the mid-seventeenth century to form the narrow Chapel of Etchmiadzin, named after a holy city in Armenia. The main feature here is the altar of Sinai containing stones from Mount Sinai, Mount Tabor and the River Jordan which provide a focus for veneration for those who are not fortunate to make a pilgrimage to these places.

Opening Times:
Monday to Friday: 15.00–15.30
Saturday and Sunday: 14.30–15.15

Telephone: (02) 282331

Church of St Mark

A Syrian Orthodox Church claimed to be on the site of the house of Mary the mother of John Mark, author of the second Gospel. If this is true then it was here that St Peter first came when he was released from prison by an angel (Acts 12. 12–17). The Syrians, sometimes known as the Assyrians, also have a tradition that this was the site of the 'Upper Room', the scene of the Feet Washing and the Last Supper.

Access

This small Church situated within its Monastery compound is difficult to find because it is in a somewhat isolated position east of the Armenian Quarter, north-west of the rebuilt Jewish Quarter, and south of David Street which runs from the Jaffa Gate towards the Temple Area. The best approach is to enter the Old City by the Jaffa Gate, follow the road round the high walls of the Citadel passing the bridge leading into the main entrance. Continue for about 150 metres and just before entering a half-arch covered passageway ahead, turn immediately left into St James Road. Follow this road round to the left and then to the right and proceed until reaching a junction. Here turn left and eventually pass through two covered passageways. At the end of the second turn right. In 25 metres, on the right, is the door leading into the compound. Ring the bell.

Tour

Inside, on the left of the low vaulted courtyard, steps lead up to the residence of the Syrian Archbishop while ahead are green double-doors leading into the Church. This is a very small Christian community and sometimes the Archbishop himself conducts visitors around the Church. He has on occasions proudly told English groups of how once he stayed in Lambeth Palace at the invitation of Archbishop Michael Ramsey.

The building dates from the Crusader period but much restoration has been carried out since the beginning of the eighteenth century. The nave walls are hung with a number of ancient religious paintings while the sanctuary is richly decorated, although sometimes partly hidden by a curtain.

Just inside the door, set into a pillar, is a stone which was discovered during restoration work in 1940 and is said to date from the sixth century. On it is an inscription written in ancient Syriac – a language very similar to Aramaic used by Our Lord. The translation is as follows:

'This is the house of Mary, mother of John, called Mark. Proclaimed a church by the holy apostles under the name of Virgin Mary, mother of God, after the ascension of our Lord Jesus Christ into heaven. Renewed after the destruction of Jerusalem by Titus in the year AD 73.'

Against the south wall of the nave is a font with an ornate canopy. Here there is an ancient portrait on parchment of the Virgin Mary which the Syrians claim was painted by St Luke himself. They also believe that the Virgin was baptised by the Holy Apostles within the original house of John Mark.

Two other significant events which, according to Syrian tradition, took place on this site are: the election of Matthias as an Apostle to replace Judas Iscariot, and the coming of the Holy Spirit on the assembled company at Pentecost.

The Church is regularly used by the small and devout Syrian (Jacobite) congregation. Some pilgrims find St Marks a fitting place from which to commence their Maundy Thursday devotional walk because it is within the City walls, and geographically is still on Mount Zion. If it is not feasible to gain admission to the Church in the evening, devotions can be conducted in the quiet street outside. Canon Ronald Brownrigg in his book 'Come, see the Place' goes so far as to suggest that, by prior arrangement, groups might be able to seek entry and also to persuade one of the Syrian priests to read the words of the institution of Communion: 'This is my body . . . This is my blood' in a language which would have been recognisable by the Apostles.

Opening Times: 8.00–15.30 (Closed on Sundays)

Telephone: (02) 283304

Ophel Archaeological Excavations

Officially called the 'Archaeological Garden' the area directly below the southern wall of the Temple platform is of particular Christian interest. The extensive excavations include the remains of a wide flight of steps which would undoubtedly have been used by Jesus when he went up to the Temple to pray and to teach.

Access

The ticket office is immediately inside the Dung Gate (see map on page xvi).

Details

Thorough excavation took place here between 1968 and 1984. Previously the eastern end had been a grassy slope where sheep were often seen grazing. Six periods of occupation have been revealed – First Temple; Hasmonean; Second Temple; Byzantine; Omayyad (early Muslim); and Medieval.

From the entrance gate only half the excavated area is visible. The south-eastern section containing the ancient steps is beyond the Ottoman wall which divides the site.

Below the south-west corner of the Temple platform further excavation of the ruins has been carried out and it is now possible to look down onto the Herodian paved street level of the deep Tyropean Valley which used to run along the west side of the platform. This valley, filled with rubble over the centuries, continued under the modern wide pavement immediately in front of the Western Wall. Here, above the ground level, seven courses of huge stone blocks form the sacred part of the wall, but below them are a further eight courses giving an idea of the depth of the valley at this point in the first century.

Also visible from the excavations, near the southern end of the western wall, is the stub of an arch which originally spanned the Tyropean Valley. This is known as 'Robinson's Arch' so named after the American archaeologist who discovered it in 1835 having removed buildings and rubble. The foundations of the western pier of the arch have also been revealed directly opposite the protruding stub.

As a matter of interest a second archway, known as 'Wilson's Arch', still exists to the north of the present sacred area of the Western Wall. It is within the buildings to the left of the pavement reserved for male worshippers. Underneath the span is a prayer hall.

The Second Temple period steps at the far end of the site gave access to the Temple Mount by way of a Double Gate in the wall which is now almost hidden by later buildings. These also cover half the width of the steps. Most of the remaining stairway has now been restored with Jerusalem stone, but a few of the steps have been left in their original state. Further along the wall to the right can be seen a triple gateway which has been filled in. This also gave access to the Temple precincts.

Authors' Comments

A visit to the excavations is very worthwhile. A detailed plan of the area is provided on admission so that the numbered features can be identified. Three routes are marked out and it is suggested that about an hour should be allowed to follow the shorter one which concentrates upon the remains of the Second Temple period and includes the ancient steps. Two hours are recommended to cover the intermediate route, and three for the longest where a total of eighteen different features can be visited.

Opening Times:
9.00–17.00 Sunday–Thursday
Friday and holiday eves closes two hours earlier
Closed on Saturday

Souvenir Shop: Postcards and books in the ticket office.

Toilets: None

Custodian: East Jerusalem Development Ltd

Mount Zion

The Dormition Abbey
The Upper Room
The Tomb of David

Mount Zion is the high ground outside the Zion Gate in the south-west corner of the Old City. See plan of Jerusalem on page xvi. It also extends into the Armenian Quarter inside the City walls.

In Our Lord's time the whole of the Mount was densely populated and enclosed within the walls. There is a tradition that the Last Supper was celebrated in an 'Upper Room' in this area. It seems likely that in a house on Zion Jesus appeared on the first Easter evening – 'the doors being shut where the Disciples were assembled for fear of the Jews'. It is also probable that on Mount Zion the Holy Spirit descended upon them at Pentecost.

During the fourth century the Roman Emperor Constantine was sufficiently convinced of the validity of these traditions to build on the Mount one of the four earliest Churches in the Holy Land which was later enlarged and known as 'Hagia Zion' – Holy Zion. The other three were the Church of the Holy Sepulchre, the one known as 'Eleona' on the Mount of Olives, and the Church of the Nativity in Bethlehem.

'Hagia Zion' was considered to be the Mother of the Churches and covered the entire area now occupied by the Church of the Dormition, the Crusader Upper Room, and the Tomb of David. Some fragments of this Church were discovered when the foundations for the

Dormition Abbey were excavated in 1906.

THE DORMITION ABBEY

The conical grey roof with the fine adjacent bell-tower is one of the most distinctive landmarks in Jerusalem. The full Latin name of the Church is 'Dormitio Sanctae Mariae' – the falling asleep

of St Mary. There is a tradition that the Virgin Mary spent the latter years of her life on Mount Zion.

Access (see map on page xvi)

From the Zion Gate in the south-west corner of the Old City, cross the road to take the promenade which runs away from the City walls and in 60 metres bear right. In a further 40 metres turn right into a narrow passageway leading to the courtyard in front of the Church. Within the Benedictine Abbey complex is a quality gift shop and a pleasant refectory where refreshments are available.

Tour

The Church was consecrated in 1910 and is in the care of an international community of German-speaking Benedictine monks. Inside, the lofty circular interior has a sense of spaciousness and the apse is dominated by a fine golden mosaic of the Virgin and Child. Portrayed below are the eight Old Testament Prophets who foretold the coming of the Messiah: Micah; Isaiah; Jeremiah; Ezekiel; Daniel; Haggai; Zechariah; and Malachi.

On either side of the apse are three chapels. Facing the altar and working clockwise from the left these are dedicated to: St Boniface, the Benedictine Archbishop; St John the Baptist; St Joseph; Maternus, the first Bishop of Cologne –

the present Bishop continues to be responsible for the Abbey; St Willibald, born in Wessex and the first known English pilgrim to the Holy Land who later became Bishop of Eichstatt; and St Benedict, the founder of the Monastic Order.

The Church is often used for concerts and on these occasions the fine round mosaic in the floor below the rotunda is hidden from view by a carpet. The design, in concentric circles, represents the spreading of the Word through time and space, emanating from the Triune God outwards via the Old and New Testaments. The three intersecting circles at the centre each contain the Greek word *Hagios* (Holy) and symbolise the Godhead. The second circle contains the names of the four major prophets and the third those of the twelve minor prophets. The four Evangelists with their appropriate symbols are next depicted, while the fifth circle contains the names of the twelve Apostles. It is interesting to note that Paul has replaced Judas. The penultimate circle shows the months of the year together with the 'Signs of the Zodiac' – pagan symbols sometimes used by Christians to represent the whole universe. Finally around the outside is a quotation in Latin from Proverbs 8.23–25: 'I was formed in earliest times, at the beginning before earth itself. I was born when there was yet no ocean, when there were no springs brimming with water. Before the mountains were settled in their place, before the hills I was born'.

On the balcony at the back of the Church is a fine modern organ built in the early 1980's by the German firm of Oberlinger Brothers.

To the right of the organ, at ground level, stairs lead down to the crypt where in the centre the prominent feature is a life-size statue of the sleeping Virgin Mary. It is carved from cherry wood and ivory. The cupola above is adorned with mosaics depicting Christ surrounded by six women of the Old Testament: Eve; Miriam; Jael; Judith; Ruth; and Esther.

There are three chapels on either side of the main altar dedicated to the memory of the Apostles. From the crypt stairs, working immediately clockwise, these are gifts from the United States; Brazil; Venezuela; Hungary; Austria; and the Ivory Coast.

Authors' Comments

Quite apart from the veneration of the Blessed Virgin Mary, this is a most suitable place in which to remember three primary events in the history of the early Church: the institution of the Last Supper; Our Lord's Resurrection

appearance to the Disciples when they were all together on Easter evening; and the coming of the Holy Spirit at Pentecost which traditionally occurred on Mount Zion.

Opening Times:
8.00–12.00 14.00–18.00 daily

Souvenir Shop:
Within the Abbey complex

Toilets:
Within the Abbey complex

Custodian: The German Society for the Holy Land. The Abbey is entrusted to an international community of German-speaking Benedictine Monks

Telephone: (02) 719927

* * *

THE UPPER ROOM

Known also as the 'Cenacle' or 'Coenaculum' (Upper Supper Room). This room, with its central pillars and gothic arches, is reminiscent of many throughout Europe in medieval abbeys and castles. Built more than a thousand years after the event which it commemorates – the Last Supper – it is most unlikely that any part dates from Apostolic times. For Christians there is no focal point for devotion, but one of the walls contains a Muslim Mihrab (prayer niche).

Access (see map on page xvi)

From the Zion Gate in the south-west corner of the Old City, cross the road to take the promenade which runs away

from the City walls and in 60 metres bear right in front of the entrance to the 'Terra Sancta' Monastery. Keep straight ahead and in about 70 metres, on the left, is a small archway leading to a flight of stone steps at the back, constructed on the outside of the building. At the top is a bare room, walk through this and into the open, then immediately ahead is the entrance to the Upper Room.

Details:

The room was part of the twelfth century Crusader Abbey and Church of Our Lady of Zion. The central pillars, of a much earlier date, have fine carved capitals. Of particular interest in the south-west corner is a slender marble column supporting a stone canopy. Carved on each face of the capital can be seen two young pelicans feeding on the blood the mother has drawn from her breast – symbolising the blood of Christ at the Eucharist.

In 1552 the Christians were expelled from the building by the Turks. Suleiman the Magnificent, who constructed the present walls of the Old City, adapted the room for Muslim worship. An inscription in arabic on the wall commemorates the event.

The ground floor of the building houses the Tomb of David and part of its surrounding walls date from the Byzantine period.

Authors' Comments

Considering the significance of the 'Upper Room' for Christians, this could possibly prove to be one of the most disappointing of all the Gospel sites in the Holy Land. No one can be certain of the exact position of the original room although it seems likely that Constantine had a very good reason for erecting one of his four Churches here on Mount Zion. Nearly all trace of his building has now been lost and it should be borne in mind that the present structure was erected as late as the twelfth century.

N.B. The Syrian Orthodox community also claim that their Church of St Mark (see page 60) is built over the authentic site of the Upper Room. Although it is well within the present City walls, it is nevertheless on the slopes of Mount Zion. Many pilgrims find it more helpful to remember the Last Supper here. The Church is not easy to find, but is situated roughly between the Cathedral of St James in the Armenian Quarter in the south-west of the Old City, and the rebuilt Jewish Quarter west of the Temple Area.

Opening Times:
The Upper Room: 8.30–16.00
Closed Friday afternoons
Souvenir Shop: None
Toilets: None

*   *   *

The Last Supper (Mark 14. 17–26)

In the evening Jesus came to the house with the Twelve. As they sat at supper he said, 'Truly I tell you: one of you will betray me – one who is eating with me.' At this they were distressed; and one by one they said to him, 'Surely you do not mean me?' 'It is one of the Twelve,' he said, 'who is dipping into the bowl with me. The Son of Man is going the way appointed for him in the scriptures; but alas for that man by whom the Son of Man is betrayed! It would be better for that man if he had never been born.

During supper he took bread, and having said the blessing he broke it and gave it to them, with the words: 'Take this; this is my body.' Then he took a cup, and having offered thanks to God he gave it to them; and they all drank from it. And he said to them, 'This is my blood, the blood of the covenant, shed for many. Truly I tell you: never again shall I drink from the fruit of the vine until that day when I drink it new in the kingdom of God.'

After singing the Passover hymn, they went out to the mount of Olives.
(REB)

'Bread becomes his Flesh from heaven,
Wine becomes his holy Blood:
Here, where sight is unavailing,
Faith may seize with grasp unfailing
What can ne'er be understood.'

For further Gospel references, see page 198

THE TOMB OF DAVID

This large sarcophagus, covered with a velvet cloth upon which stand Torah scroll-boxes and crowns is situated in a narrow room directly below the Crusader Upper Room. The building therefore is a place of pilgrimage for Jews, Muslims and Christians.

Access

Follow the instructions on page 66 for reaching the 'Upper Room' as far as: '. . . small archway'. Instead of turning through this to reach the Upper Room, continue on up the steps and pass under the tall archway ahead, and then in 15 metres turn left again. The entrance to the tomb complex is through a doorway on the left.

Details

The Jews consider this holy place second in importance to that of the Western Wall of the Temple Area. It is necessary for men to cover their heads, and prayer caps (Kippahs) are available just inside to the right of the entrance door. From here proceed directly into a smaller room which serves as an annexe to the tomb and is used for prayer.

There is some doubt about the validity of the tomb because in the Old Testament it is clearly stated that King David and his ancestors were buried in the City of David (1 Kings 2.10). This was directly south of the Temple platform and is now known as Mount Ophel. Another school of thought places the burials in Bethlehem because this town is mentioned in the New Testament as the 'City of David' (Luke 2.4). However, excavations have not revealed the royal necropolis in either location.

The earliest reference to the tomb in its present position is made by the historian Josephus in the first century. In 1173 Rabbi Benjamin of Tudela describes the tomb as one of Judaism's holiest shrines. In 1859 the Italian engineer Pierotty was granted permission to investigate the tomb and he reported that underneath was a small, shallow, and empty cave.

Authors' Comments

A Jewish Holy Place of some significance. The wall at the back of the tomb could possibly date from the early Christian 'Hagia Zion' Church.

Opening Times:
8.00–Sunset

The Church of St Peter in Gallicantu

St Peter and the Cock-Crowing

This modern Church on the eastern slope of Mount Zion is built over a reputed site of the house of the High Priest Caiaphas. It commemorates St Peter's denial of Jesus after his arrest in the Garden of Gethsemane and his subsequent remorse. There are four levels: the Upper Church; the Middle Church; the Guardroom; and the Dungeon.

Access

From the Tomb of David: Turn left into a small courtyard. The way out is diagonally opposite. Walk along the cloister towards the Museum but just before reaching it turn into a rather dark entrance on the left. Immediately opposite, though hidden from view, another door leads out into a small 'garden' opening onto the road. Turn right along this road and at the end bear round to the left in order to reach the main road. Here turn left again (towards the City walls) and in a short distance take the turning on the right which leads down to the Church. Beyond the coach and car park is a booth where admission tickets can be purchased.

modern-day Silwan, the intersection of the Kidron and Hinnom valleys, and on a clear day the Mountains of Moab in Jordan. Three panels identify the features. The houses of Silwan tightly packed together afford some idea of how the City of Jerusalem here on Mount Zion might have looked in Our Lord's time.

The Belvedere

Before turning left down to the Church it is well worth going out onto the Belvedere to enjoy the extensive views. The panorama includes the Temple Mount and the southern wall of the Old City, the Mount of Olives,

The Main Site

The validity of this site has sometimes been questioned because it is thought that such an important person as the High Priest would have had his residence in a more commanding position at the top of Mount Zion. There is some documentary evidence dating back to the fifth century of a Church in the area dedicated to St Peter, but its exact position is not stated. At the top of the Mount, near the Dormition Abbey, is a site owned by the Armenians which has not been extensively excavated. Some believe that this is more likely to have been the position of the house of the High Priest.

The Church was built in the 1920s by the French Assumptionists and consecrated in 1931. There are many features which support their claim that it is on the site of the house of the High Priest Caiaphas. These are mentioned here before proceeding further.

Excavations have revealed the remains of a substantial building with its own water cistern, corn mill, store-rooms, and servants' quarters. More importantly, a number of artefacts have been discovered including a complete set of measures for liquids and solids as used by the priests in the Temple. Also a door lintel with the word 'Korban' (sin offering) inscribed in Hebrew, together with coins, pottery and glass dating back to the Second Temple period. One of the lower levels contains what could have been a guardroom and the other what might have been a prisoners' cell. The walls of the latter have been inscribed with crosses which

the Assumptionist Fathers claim are Byzantine and indicate that the place was reverenced by Christians during this period.

Tour

(A) *The Upper Church* is approached through a new entrance porch. Immediately inside on the right of this are two Byzantine mosaics, one of them still in its original position. Ahead, doors lead into the Upper Church which is extensively decorated with mosaics. The scene above the high altar shows the 'trial' before Caiaphas.

From the entrance porch, directly opposite the two Byzantine mosaics, stairs lead down to the lower levels.

(B) *The Middle Church* has been carefully adapted to provide groups with another place for worship. Three modern ikons above the altars depict St Peter's denial, his repentance, and his reconciliation with his Master on the Galilean shore after the Resurrection. The natural bedrock of Mount Zion forms the west wall of the middle Church. It is thought possible that this level might have been the area where prisoners were interrogated.

In the floor is an ancient shaft giving access to what was possibly a small deep dungeon below. This opening would have been its only entrance necessitating the prisoner being raised by means of a

71

rope harness. There is a mosaic depicting Jesus in such a harness outside on the south wall of the Church. Three crosses dating from the Byzantine period are cut into the side of the shaft and these, together with others in the dungeon, confirm an early Christian presence.

(C) *The 'Guardroom'* can be found down the stairway at the next level. From the entrance descend the steps. The entire area has been hewn out of the bedrock; the original chisel marks are clearly visible and the floor has not been levelled.

It seems most likely that this was indeed a Jewish prison. In such a place there was no need for individual cells, or to pay much attention to the floor, because under their law offenders were not given long terms of imprisonment. They were brought in and shackled to the walls. Corporal punishment, usually in the form of scourging, was swiftly administered. The maximum number of lashes allowed was 40, but in order to avoid breaking the law by possibly miscounting, 39 were given, or as St Paul puts it: 'forty stripes save one' (2 Corinthians 11.24). The relatively few prisoners actually awaiting trial for serious crimes would have been detained in a more secure communal cell which in this instance was on a lower level.

Walk across to look between the two central pillars on the right. On one pillar and on the wall at the back are tethering loops cut into the rock through which the prisoner's chains might have been passed. At the base of the pillars are two basins hewn out of the bedrock. It is suggested that these would have contained salt to cleanse the wounds after scourging, and vinegar to revive the offender.

It should be remembered that Jesus was not scourged by the Jews because the accusation against him was much more serious: that of claiming to be the Son of God. It is suggested therefore that he was put in the dungeon overnight before appearing in front of Caiaphas who was anxious that he should be crucified. The death sentence could only be authorised by the Roman Procurator, Pontius Pilate, and it was therefore under Roman jurisdiction that Jesus was scourged in the Praetorium.

However, it seems quite likely that St Peter, and possibly some of the other Disciples, may have been scourged in this place because, according to the Acts of the Apostles, after the Resurrection they were accused of 'preaching Christ' in the Temple and this was an offence against the religious authority.

Now proceed to the back of the guardroom down a step

and then turn to the left. In the wall is an opening and directly below it a stone block which has been carved out of the bedrock. From this elevated position there is a good view through the aperture directly onto the dungeon. Thus it would have been possible for just one man to observe those in the 'Guardroom' and at the same time keep an eye on anyone in the cell below.

To reach this cell return to the entrance and turn right. Further flights of steps lead down to this lower level.

(D) *The Dungeon:* Above is the shaft into the cell which was visible earlier from the Middle Church. High up in one wall is the opening which allowed the gaoler to keep watch from the 'Guardroom'.

Around the walls are some rather faint Byzantine crosses painted in red. There are seven in all and these, together with the three crosses actually cut into the rock face of the entrance shaft, are said to date from the fifth century. High above the altar are the remains of a flight of steps of uncertain date. Psalm 88 is especially suitable to read here and also the account of Jeremiah being cast into a similar pit. The Biblical text includes a graphic description of his being raised in a rope harness. (Jeremiah 38.6–13).

Leave the dungeon and continue through the marked exit to view other features of interest outside. Below the east wall of the Church are the excavated remains of the cellars, storerooms and cistern, of what is believed to have been the house of the High Priest. It was here that many of the artefacts mentioned earlier were discovered.

Finally, on the north side of the complex are the ancient steps which were part of a main street running between the Kidron Valley and the Upper City at the top of Mount Zion. They date from not later than the Second Temple period, but were only uncovered in 1931. They would undoubtedly have been familiar to Jesus and his Disciples, and it is most likely that after arresting him in the Garden of Gethsemane the Temple Guard would have brought him up by this route for his interrogation before Caiaphas – even if the position of the High Priest's house was higher up at the top of Mount Zion.

Authors' Comments

Whether or not one accepts that St Peter in Gallicantu is built over the true site of the House of Caiaphas, the existence of a possible 'guardroom' and a 'prisoners' cell' afford an excellent visual aid to the events of Maundy Thursday night. To recall those events here, and to see the ancient steps of the City of

73

Our Lord's time can indeed be a memorable and rewarding experience.

At the time of writing extensive alterations are taking place but plans for these are not complete. We have endeavoured to be as accurate as possible in the light of the information available.

Opening Times:
8.30–12.00 14.00–17.00
(Closed on Sundays)

Souvenir Shop: Opposite the west facade of the Church on the upper path level. Well stocked containing quality gifts and books. Refreshments available.

Toilets: At the top of the stairs inside the Gift Shop

Custodian: The Assumptionists

Telephone: (02) 731739

Peter's denial (Luke 22. 54–62)

Then they arrested Jesus and led him away. They brought him to the high priest's house, and Peter followed at a distance. They lit a fire in the middle of the courtyard and sat round it, and Peter sat among them. A serving-maid who saw him sitting in the firelight stared at him and said, 'This man was with him too.' But he denied it: 'I do not know him,' he said. A little later a man noticed him and said, 'You also are one of them.' But Peter said to him, 'No, I am not.' About an hour passed and someone else spoke more strongly still: 'Of course he was with him. He must have been; he is a Galilean. But Peter said, 'I do not know what you are talking about.' At that moment, while he was still speaking, a cock crowed; and the Lord turned and looked at Peter. Peter remembered the Lord's words, 'Tonight before the cock crows you will disown me three times.' And he went outside, and wept bitterly. (REB)

'How many times with faithless word
have we denied his holy name,
How oft forsaken our dear Lord,
and shrunk when trial came.'

For further Gospel references, see page 196

Pool of Siloam

For the past 2,700 years the waters from the Spring of Gihon have flowed through Hezekiah's Tunnel to supply the Pool of Siloam. Jesus sent the man who had been blind from birth to the Pool to bathe his eyes and receive sight. In his time Siloam was an extensive reservoir serving the inhabitants of the densely populated City above, but today all that remains is a narrow watercourse in a cutting between high walls.

Access *(see map p. xvi)*

The Pool of Siloam (*Shiloah* in Hebrew) lies outside the walls on the south side of the Old City and about 400 metres from the Dung Gate.

1. *On foot:* Walk down the road immediately opposite the Gate keeping round to the left. Descend the steep slope and, almost immediately after it joins another road, look out on the left for a break in the wall where steps lead down to the entrance. The minaret of a Mosque directly behind the Pool will be clearly visible.

2. *By car:* From the Jaffa or the Damascus Gate drive round the Old City walls in a clockwise direction until reaching the far south-eastern corner where the massive stones tower above the roadway. Continue on round the walls for a short distance and look out for a road on the left beside a car and coach park. Descend this road for about 450 metres and then on the left will be seen the minaret of a Mosque which is directly behind the Pool. Park nearby and walk down some steps to the entrance.

Details

Enter through a doorway in the surrounding wall on the left. Inside on the right is a kiosk selling souvenirs. For a small donation the owner may unlock the iron gates leading down to the Pool. Descend the 32 stone steps to the water level and ahead will be seen, through an archway, the southern end of Hezekiah's Tunnel. The water flowing through it comes from the Spring of Gihon which wells up at the other end outside the line of the ancient City walls. The tunnel is 533

Jesus gives sight to a man born blind (John 9. 1–12)

As he went on his way Jesus saw a man who had been blind from birth. His disciples asked him, 'Rabbi, why was this man born blind? Who sinned, this man or his parents?' 'It is not that he or his parents sinned,' Jesus answered; 'he was born blind so that God's power might be displayed in curing him. While daylight lasts we must carry on the work of him who sent me; night is coming, when no one can work. While I am in the world I am the light of the world.'

With these words he spat on the ground and made a paste with the spittle; he spread it on the man's eyes, and said to him, 'Go and wash in the pool of Siloam. (The name means 'Sent'.) The man went off and washed, and came back able to see.

His neighbours and those who were accustomed to see him begging said, 'Is not this the man who used to sit and beg?' Some said, 'Yes, it is.' Others said, 'No, but it is someone like him.' He himself said, 'I am the man.' They asked him, 'How were your eyes opened?' He replied, 'The man called Jesus made a paste and smeared my eyes with it, and told me to go to Siloam and wash. So I went and washed, and found I could see.' 'Where is he?' they asked. 'I do not know,' he said. (REB)

'Let thy glorious light
shine ever on my sight,
and clothe me round,
the while my path illuming.'

metres long and was hewn out of the solid rock in the seventh century BC by Hezekiah, King of Judah. He thereby ensured that even when under siege Jerusalem had its own fresh water supply within the confines of the City. If nobody is walking through the tunnel the water is clear, otherwise it can become very cloudy at the pool end.

Notice in the water some of the remains of the columns from a fifth century Byzantine Church which stood on this site and was destroyed by the Persians in AD 614. Today the Pool is a mere channel only fifteen metres long and two metres wide. Immediately above are the walls of a Mosque built about 100 years ago.

In Our Lord's time the water from the Pool of Siloam played an important part in the Feast of Tabernacles. On the last day of the Festival it was ceremonially carried up to the Temple in a golden ewer and poured out by the High Priest on the great Altar of Sacrifice. It is thought that Jesus had just witnessed this ceremony when he spoke the words recorded in St John's Gospel (7.37) 'If anyone is thirsty let him come to me and drink'.

Authors' Comments

Although there are no accurate records of its shape and size 2,000 years ago, it was undoubtedly much larger then.

Opening Times: When the custodian is in attendance

Souvenir Shop: On the site

Toilets: None

Custodian: The Muslims. A small donation is required to descend the steps to the water

Spring of Gihon

Hezekiah's Tunnel and
Warren's Shaft

THE SPRING OF GIHON

Situated in the Kidron Valley 300 metres due south of the south-east corner of the Temple Area (see map on page 4). At the time of writing the road is blocked to vehicles at the Gethsemane end of the valley and it is unwise to descend to the site on foot unaccompanied.

Approaching from the north, the entrance to the underground spring is on the right of the road running along the bottom of the valley, just beyond a school playground and beneath a fairly modern house. Thirty three steps lead down to the water which wells up in a rock cavern. A tunnel dating possibly from 1800 BC runs off westwards and used to take the water to a point directly under the ancient city. It was then hauled up in buckets via a deep shaft, now known as 'Warren's Shaft' (see details opposite). It is thought most likely that, circa 1000 BC, this was the shaft up which King David's men climbed in order to capture the city (2 Samuel 5. 6–8; 1 Chronicles 11. 4–9). The spring was the only fresh water source in Jerusalem and here Zadok the Priest and Nathan the Prophet anointed Solomon King of Israel (1 Kings 1. 38–40).

HEZEKIAH'S TUNNEL

At the beginning of the eighth century BC, Hezekiah King of Judah, accomplished a remarkable feat by extending part of the original tunnel for a distance of over half a kilometre. (2 Kings 20.20; 2 Chronicles 32.30). Following a natural fissure, the winding conduit was hewn out of solid rock to bring the spring water within the city to the Pool of Siloam (see page 75) which then served as a reservoir. The workmen started cutting from both ends and it is interesting to note that the roof from the Siloam entrance is higher because when the two teams eventually met the floor had to be lowered at that end to allow the water to flow. The axe and chisel marks can be seen along the entire length and in some places there are signs that the workmen started to cut slightly off course. After completion of the work the Gihon end was then hidden from view because it was vulnerable to attack during a siege.

As recently as 1880 an ancient Hebrew inscription was discovered engraved in the rock of the tunnel commemorating the fact that the workmen achieved their objective. This chunk of original wall was removed and is now displayed in the Archaeological Museum in Istanbul. A replica has now been placed in the tunnel.

A feature of the Gihon spring is that it gushes out in great volume for about half an hour and then hardly flows at all for many hours (the name Gihon means 'gushing'). Generally the water level in the tunnel is about knee-high but when in full flow it can reach the lower part of the body. However at two points it is even deeper.

Before wading through the tunnel, an entrance fee must be negotiated at either the Gihon or the Siloam end. Candles will probably be supplied but they are likely to blow out so a torch is essential. Canvas shoes should also be worn. The passage is very narrow and in places it is just possible to pass another person.

WARREN'S SHAFT

So named after the English archaeologist Charles Warren who in 1867 discovered this ancient subterranean access to the spring water. The most recent excavation took place under the direction of the Israeli Archaeologist Yigal Shiloh between 1978 and 1982 when all the rubble was removed so that it is now possible to walk down the wide underground approach to the top of the shaft. This is

very worthwhile and one is reminded of the tunnel hewn out of the rock to reach a similar water source at Megiddo in Northern Israel, but the approach is very steep and hazardous towards the end.

Access (see map p. xvi)

Very few tourist maps show the location of Warren's shaft which is only approachable on foot. It is best to start from the Dung Gate in the southern wall of the Old City. Cross the main road outside the gate and turn left to walk downhill parallel to the walls. Turn first right into a road running south beside the coach and car park. Proceed for about 100 metres and then look out for a tarmacadam path on the left beside a wall. Walk along this, turn right at the end descending a series of steps which lead directly to the City of David Archaeological Garden containing the excavated Jebusite walls of the ancient city. Here turn right and descend one series of steps and then left to descend further steps. Halfway down descend a further flight of steps on the right onto the approach path to Warren's Shaft which runs parallel to the Kidron Valley but may not be well marked.

There is an admission fee. Descend the steep spiral staircase to a small exhibition area and then follow the signs. Further long flights of steps have to be negotiated to reach the wide tunnel some thirty metres in length, which itself is fairly steep and rough underfoot in places. The ancient shaft at the end is thirteen metres deep and the water below can be heard if the Gihon Spring is in full flow.

Opening Times:
Sunday to Thursday: 9.00–17.00
Friday and holiday eves: 9.00–13.00
Closed on Saturday
The admission charge is reduced for groups

Telephone: (02) 288141

Bethlehem

The main feature of this world-famous town is the Church of the Nativity built over the cave where, according to a very strong and unchallenged tradition, Jesus was born. The existing building dates from the latter part of the sixth century and is Christendom's oldest complete church.

Access

Bethlehem lies 8 km south of Jerusalem on the main Hebron/Beersheba road. After about 5 km notice on the left the Greek Orthodox Monastery of Mar Elias where it is claimed the Prophet Elijah rested. From here one has the first view of the 'Little Town of Bethlehem' – still quite small by modern standards. Soon after entering the outskirts of the town look out on the right for Rachel's Tomb, a place of pilgrimage for Jews and Muslims. Be sure to take the left fork at a small roundabout soon

afterwards and then remain on this road, ignoring all turnings to the left, in order to reach the Church of the Nativity and Manger Square.

THE TOWN

Bethlehem is likely to be among the first places visited on a pilgrimage before one has had time to become accustomed to Arab culture and living standards. A word of warning therefore to the Christian pilgrim who may have been conditioned from a very early age by children's carols and Christmas cribs. The town can come as quite a shock to those who, perhaps less than twenty four hours earlier, were still in England:

– It is a relatively poor and untidy place even compared with Jerusalem and the sharp contrast between the East and the West is very pronounced.

– It is a mecca, not only for Christians, but for millions of tourists who flock here from all over the world. Occasionally, the little town can suddenly be inundated by passengers from a cruise ship calling in at Haifa. The only consolation being that these large parties do not stay very long.

– Pilgrims sometimes feel that there is too much commercialism, but this is only because practically everyone wishes to take home a souvenir of their visit. A desire which is even stronger in Christians. Consequently, be prepared for competitive street trading and realise that most of the shops are dependent upon the tourist. There is no trading within the Church of the Nativity – which is more than can be said for many Cathedrals and Parish Churches in England.

In addition to the Church of the Nativity, there are many other churches, monasteries, convents and orphanages in the town. Try to visit the market which is frequented by Bedouin from the desert around. To reach this, walk due west from the Church of the Nativity, cross Manger Square and take the street to the right of the Tourist Information Office and then ascend a flight of steps. In this area there are no tourist shops and the streets nearby have changed very little in two thousand years.

Bethlehem is renowned for its olive wood carvings and mother of pearl souvenirs. Some of these are made by craftsmen in the little shops along Milk Grotto Street which is to the right of the Church of the Nativity.

THE CHURCH OF THE NATIVITY

Historical Evidence

Although there is no actual mention in the Gospels of Jesus being born in a cave, even today one can see primitive shepherd dwellings in these Judaean hills where families live directly above a cave which provides natural shelter for their animals.

Certainly local people would have remembered the birth – not least the shepherds who must often have been asked by their children, and their grandchildren, to tell the story of how the angels appeared to them on that first Christmas night. Their descendants would have known exactly where the birth took place.

The visit of the Magi must also have been a memorable event.

The oral tradition was undoubtedly very strong and in AD 135 the Roman Emperor Hadrian, perhaps to divert attention from the site, gave orders that a grove, dedicated to the pagan god Adonis, should be planted in the immediate vicinity of the cave. If, as St Jerome suggests, this really was his intention, in effect he marked its location for the next two hundred years. The earliest written reference to the Bethlehem cave, surrounded by a grove dedicated to Adonis, was made by the Christian missionary Justin Martyr in AD 155. The writer Origen also confirms the same tradition in AD 215.

In 315 the Emperor Constantine, having been converted to Christianity by his mother St Helena, directed that a magnificent Basilica should be erected over the cave. His building stood for two hundred years before being extensively

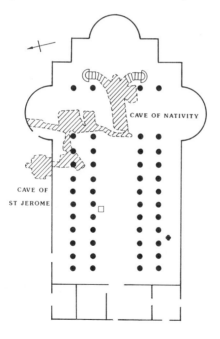

Church of The Nativity
showing part of cave complex

damaged in the Samaritan Revolts during the first half of the sixth century. Later during that same century the Emperor Justinian erected a larger Basilica on the site incorporating parts of Constantine's structure. This building has survived to the present day.

Tour

It is important to realise that the sixth century building is today owned jointly by the Greek Orthodox and Armenian Churches and thus the interior reflects the Eastern tradition. In contrast, the comparatively modern Roman Catholic Church of St Catherine, built adjacent to the north wall of the ancient Basilica, is more in keeping with the Western tradition.

Cross the road from Manger Square and pause to identify how the buildings are integrated. Immediately on the right is the Armenian Convent with its rather squat modern bell-tower. Further along on the right can be seen the top of the much larger tower belonging to the Greek Orthodox Convent, while the Roman Catholic tower, from which the bells are sometimes broadcast on Christmas Eve, is on the left. However, from this position it is hidden from view by the fortress-like west front of the main Church.

Before entering the building, pause again to observe the three earlier doorways which have now been filled in. The highest arch dates from the sixth century. Immediately across this is a lintel which was constructed some time later. Much further down is a twelfth century arch built by the Crusaders, while finally the very low doorway was made by the Turks in the sixteenth century. These entrances were reduced in size solely for defensive purposes, but for the Christian there is the rather profound thought that everyone, but a child, has to bow the head in order to enter the birthplace of Jesus.

This is the oldest complete church in the world. According to a legend documented as early as AD 838, when the Persians destroyed all the Christian buildings in the Holy Land at the beginning of the seventh century, they recognised on this west facade a representation of the Magi in costumes of their own country. Thus in respect and reverence for their ancestors they spared the Basilica from destruction.

Now stoop to enter the low doorway and after passing through a rather dark narthex, stop to survey the interior which has changed very little since the Emperor Justinian constructed it. In accordance with the Eastern Orthodox tradition the nave is completely devoid of furniture. The fine red limestone columns were quarried locally, while it is said that some of the roof timbers were a gift from King Edward III of England in the fourteenth century. The main altar is hidden from view by a large wooden screen, known as an iconostasis, ornately carved and adorned with ikons. Before moving on look back to see the heavy wooden entrance door made by an Armenian carpenter in 1227.

Next turn right to examine the ancient Justinian font in the south aisle. Now turn back into the centre of the nave to view, about half a metre below the present floor level, a section of the exceptionally fine mosaic from the original floor of Constantine's Church dating from AD 325. Notice also high up on the walls some remains of much later mosaics with which the Crusaders lavishly adorned the Church in the twelfth century.

On Christmas Day AD 1100 their first King, Baldwin I, was crowned here. Godfrey de Bouillon, who had previously been elected King of Jerusalem, refused this title but became 'Defender of the Holy Sepulchre' saying: 'How can I accept a crown of gold in the place where my Saviour was crowned with thorns?'

Before proceeding further, stand in the middle of the nave facing the Greek iconostasis. The Cave of the Nativity is directly below the platform in front of this screen. Originally, Constantine built an octagonal structure over the cave from which it was possible for worshippers to look down directly into the place of birth.

Mount the steps of the platform, and pause to reflect that beneath one's feet is the sacred place where the Son of God was born.

Now turn right into the south transept. The altar against the east wall belongs to the Greek Orthodox Church and commemorates the Circumcision. The steps beside the iconostasis lead down to the cave. If there is a queue try to wait until the way is clear as the majority of groups pass through very quickly. It may also be helpful to have some idea of the layout of the cave before entering:

The Place of the Nativity

– The cave is rectangular and measures approximately 11 metres by 3 metres.
– Immediately to the left at the bottom of the steps, at a lower level than the main floor, is a representation of the Manger.
– Between the staircases there is a small apse which has an altar built into it. Underneath, set in the floor, is a silver star marking the traditional place of birth.
– The other steps also lead up into the Church.

Since the sixth century the

walls of the cave have been lined with marble in order to preserve them. They in turn are protected by heavy leather drapes backed with asbestos following a serious fire in 1869. The holes in these drapes allow the ceiling lamps to be lowered. Nevertheless, depending upon how elaborately the cave is decorated, it may be possible to see small sections of the natural rock. The roof has been blackened by the burning of candles for over fourteen hundred years.

On Feast Days the cave is lit by 48 hanging lamps, 21 of them belonging to the Roman Catholic Church. At Christmas a lifesize effigy of the Holy Babe is placed in the Manger. The small altar opposite it is dedicated to the Magi.

Pause to reflect that the Church is open for twelve hours each day and during this time the cave is rarely empty. It is probably true to say that more prayers have been offered up from this hallowed place than from anywhere else in Christendom.

Leave the cave by ascending the steps to the left of the star which lead into the north transept of the Church. This area belongs to the Armenians. The altar immediately to the right is dedicated to the Three Kings, while the one straight ahead honours the Virgin. Beside the

---

The Birth of Jesus (Luke 2. 1–7)

And it came to pass in those days, that there went out a decree from Caesar Augustus, that all the world should be taxed. (And this taxing was first made when Cyrenius was governor of Syria). And all went to be taxed, every one into his own city. And Joseph also went up from Galilee, out of the city of Nazareth, into Judaea, unto the city of David, which is called Bethlehem, (because he was of the house and lineage of David). To be taxed with Mary his espoused wife, being great with child. And so it was, that, while they were there, the days were accomplished that she should be delivered. And she brought forth her firstborn son, and wrapped him in swaddling clothes, and laid him in a manger; because there was no room for them in the inn. (AV)

'I come, I bring, I offer here
All Thou to me hast given.
Take then, dear Lord, my mind and heart,
My spirit, soul, and every part,
For all I offer gladly.'

For further Gospel references, see page 195

raised platform in front of the Greek iconostasis are trapdoors in the floor under which can be seen the remains of other fine mosaics from the Constantinian Church. Now pass through the north door into:

The Church of St Catherine

This Roman Catholic Church, greatly enlarged from the original Crusader building was constructed in 1882 and further extended in 1949. It is from here that Midnight Mass is sometimes broadcast on Christmas Eve. Notice the design of the nave lighting in the form of catherine wheels. In the south aisle 29 steps lead down to:

The Cave of St Jerome

This cave is of considerable importance for two reasons. Firstly, it was here that from AD 386–404 St Jerome laboured to translate the Bible from Hebrew and Greek into Latin. His version, known as The Vulgate, is still used by the Roman Catholic Church. He was assisted by two pious ladies, St Paula and her daughter St Eustochium who, together with St Jerome founded Christian monastic communities around Bethlehem.

Secondly, the cave is beneath the Church of the Nativity and is also directly connected to the place of birth. The underground caverns were carefully reinstated by the Franciscans in 1964, so that now one has a very clear idea of what the Cave of the Nativity could have looked like before it was lined with marble in the sixth century.

Tour

From the bottom of the narrow steps into the first cavern, look to the left and notice a half-arch which is part of the Constantinian foundation of the Church of the Nativity. Further around on the left is an altar and a number of first and second century sarcophagi some of which are reputed to be those of the Holy Innocents. The main feature here is a raised altar commemorating St Joseph's dream in which the angel instructed him to take Mary and the Babe and hasten into Egypt. Immediately to the right of the altar is a narrow passage, reputedly cut by St Jerome, so that he could have direct access to the Cave of the Nativity.

Walk under an archway, close to the entrance steps, which leads into two smaller caverns. In the first, on the right, is an altar dedicated to St Eusebius, a disciple of St Jerome, while on the left is an ancient cistern. Notice how the rim has been worn by the rubbing of ropes. A little further on in the next cavern is an altar dedicated to St Paula and St Eustochium, whilst ahead is the cenotaph of St Jerome himself.

Finally, walk through another narrow passageway to the Chapel of St Jerome. In this room he is said to have produced The Vulgate. At the back of the chapel, behind a glass door with an ornate grille, is a flight of steps which leads directly up into the cloister in front of St Catherine's Church.

Now return to the Church of St Catherine and go out by the west door into a delightful cloister dedicated to St Jerome whose statue, made of terra cotta and mounted on a granite column, provides a fitting centrepiece.

Opening Times:
The Church of the Nativity
6.00–18.00 daily
Church of St Catherine
5.00–12.00 14.00–18.00 daily

Souvenir Shop: None

Toilets: None

Custodians:
The Church of the Nativity
The Armenians and the Greek Orthodox
Church of St Catherine
The Roman Catholics

Telephone:
St Catherine's: (02) 742425

Other Christian buildings in the vicinity

The Armenian and Greek Orthodox Convents adjoin the Church. The latter is reached through the door in the south transept. The Armenian Convent can be approached by going through the south door of the dark entrance-narthex of the Church.

Nearby in Milk Grotto Street which runs east from Manger Square is the church built over the shrine of the 'Milk Grotto'. The entrance is 250 metres along on the right. It is so called because, according to a sixth century legend, when the Virgin Mary was suckling the baby Jesus here a drop of her milk fell onto the ground and the rock immediately turned white. Pieces of the rock can be seen as relics in many Churches throughout the world because it is claimed to have therapeutic qualities.

Even today some young women come here to pray to the Holy Mother for a plentiful supply of milk for their babes. The present shrine was built by the Franciscans in 1871 and parts of it are lavishly decorated with mother of pearl.

Opening Times:
Milk Grotto:
8.00–11.15 14.00–16.30 daily.
Ring the bell

Telephone: (02) 743867

THE SHEPHERDS' FIELDS

There are two principal sites which commemorate the appearance of the angels to the shepherds on that first Christmas night. Where precisely this event occurred is unknown, but the exact location is quite unimportant because anywhere down here, at the bottom of the hill from the little town, it is easy to imagine the shepherds tending their sheep. Although many of the fields are now cultivated, sheep can still be seen nibbling the scanty pasture by the roadside.

The older site of the two is near the distinctive modern red-domed Greek Orthodox Church which was finally completed in 1989. Here there are remains of a fourth century church, the crypt of which was regularly used by the Orthodox Community prior to the opening of the new building. The latter contains a beautiful iconostasis and many other fine examples of modern art and craftsmanship. If time permits it is well worth a visit.

The alternative site is owned by the Franciscans and the view from it is probably more in keeping with the Western idea of what the fields would have looked like two thousand years ago. There is a pleasant garden which provides an ideal setting in which to meditate upon the Christmas story. This location is described in detail overpage.

Access

In order to reach the Franciscan compound which is 2½ km from the town, depart from Manger Square by the main road. In 50 metres turn right where signposted 'Shepherds' Fields'. Descend the steep hill for nearly 1 km and turn left at the sign 'Welcome to the Shepherds' Fields', then keep to the left down the hill. On reaching the crossroads keep straight on. Ahead, among the trees is the Franciscan compound.

To visit the Greek Orthodox site continue on past the Franciscan compound for a further 250 metres. Turn right onto the main road, and on the left can be seen the red domes of the modern Church. To reach it turn first left off the main road, then first left again.

Tour of the Franciscan Site

From the entrance gate there is a pleasant walk of about 150 metres to the main compound. At the end on the left are the remains of a Byzantine agricultural monastery. From here there is a fine view across the barren countryside. In the distance are the modern suburbs of Jerusalem, but in the foreground one can see caves where the shepherds still shelter. Of particular interest is a track winding around the hillside because it is probable that this was used by Joseph and Mary if, as St Luke suggests, they journeyed from Nazareth. The track by-passes Jerusalem on the way up from the Jordan Valley. Although the Jordan route was longer than going through Samaria, the journey would have been easier for Mary in her condition, and the road less prone to attack from brigands.

The traditional shepherd still leads his sheep, rather than drives them from behind as in England. Each man has a distinctive call which his flock recognises. Jesus said: 'The sheep hear the shepherd's voice; he calls his own sheep by name, and leads them out. When he has brought them all out, he goes ahead of them and the sheep follow, because they know his voice . . . I am the good shepherd; I know my own and my own know me'. (John 10.3a–4 & 14)

Follow the boundary railing round, and on the left is a gate which leads down to a secluded area where an altar has been erected among the Byzantine ruins. Ahead are the remains of a tower which has been converted into the Custodian's residence. In the foreground is a cave, and a little further to the right is a larger one, now protected by an entrance door, which has been set out as a chapel. Notice within how the ceiling has been blackened by the shepherds' fires since time immemorial.

Finally, follow a path which leads up to the Chapel of the Angels. This expressive building designed by the Italian Architect, Antonio Barluzzi, represents a bedouin tent. The foundation stone was laid on Christmas Day 1953 and the chapel was consecrated exactly a year later. There is a fine bronze casting of an angel above the entrance door. Inside, four figures support the central altar, while the light floods through the dome symbolising the heavenly light which surrounded the angels on that first Christmas night. Three small apses contain delightful paintings depicting the scenes.

Opening Times
8.00–11.30 14.00–17.30 daily (Winter: 17.00)

Souvenir Shop: None. (Beware of persistent traders outside the gate)

Toilets: On the left at the end of the entrance path

Custodian: The Franciscans

Telephone: (02) 6472413

The Story of the Shepherds (Luke 2. 8–20)

And there were in the same country shepherds abiding in the field, keeping watch over their flock by night. And, lo, the angel of the Lord came upon them, and the glory of the Lord shone round about them: and they were sore afraid. And the angel said unto them, 'Fear not: for, behold, I bring you good tidings of great joy, which shall be to all people. For unto you is born this day, in the city of David, a Saviour, which is Christ the Lord. And this shall be a sign unto you: Ye shall find the babe wrapped in swaddling clothes, lying in a manger'. And suddenly there was with the angel a multitude of the heavenly host, praising God, and saying, 'Glory to God in the highest, and on earth peace, good will toward men'.

And it came to pass, as the angels were gone away from them into heaven, the shepherds said one to another, 'Let us now go even unto Bethlehem, and see this thing which is come to pass, which the Lord hath made known unto us'. And they came with haste, and found Mary, and Joseph, and the babe lying in a manger. And when they had seen it, they made known abroad the saying which was told them concerning this child. And all they that heard it wondered at those things which were told them by the shepherds. But Mary kept all these things, and pondered them in her heart. And the shepherds returned, glorifying and praising God for all the things that they had heard and seen, as it was told unto them. (AV)

'While the angels in the sky
Sang praise above the silent field,
To shepherds poor the Lord most high,
The one great Shepherd, was revealed.'

The Herodion

Herod the Great adapted the summit of a mountain in the barren Judaean hills to create another of his private fortified palaces. This particular location however must have been rather special to him as he named it after himself and expressed the wish that upon his death he should be buried there. Today it resembles an extinct volcano and can be seen in the distance to the left of the Jerusalem/Bethlehem road. At the foot of the mountain he also constructed a number of other buildings including a separate palace for the reception and accommodation of guests. The complex also comprised a large rectangular pool surrounded by attractive gardens.

Access

From Jerusalem: Distance about 20 km. From the Jaffa Gate take the main road to Bethlehem but after 5 km look out on the left for the prominent Mar Elias Monastery. Soon after passing this turn left just *before* the traffic lights, and then almost immediately right. In 1½ km at the junction turn right, and then drive on for 5 km until reaching crossroads which are at the summit of a hill*. Here continue straight ahead to the next T-junction and turn left.

Soon afterwards at the bottom of the hill take the right fork uphill. In 3 km bear right by a mosque. The Herodion is about 2 km from here and is clearly visible to the left. When almost parallel to the mountain look out for a number of re-erected Roman pillars beside the road and then almost immediately take the road to the left. The car park, toilets and ticket office are near the top of the mountain.

From Bethlehem: Depart from Manger Square and in 50 metres turn right where signposted 'Shepherds' Fields'. Keep straight ahead down this road for 1 km and take the left fork. In another 1½ km take the left fork again signposted 'Jericho'. Continue on this road for a further 2 km and at the crossroads turn right. Then follow the access instructions from Jerusalem after the* on page 92.

History

Around 25 BC Herod began the construction of this mountain fortress by creating an artificial mound on the top of a natural peak. He then surmounted the earthworks with a circular defensive wall into which were built four towers. Three of them were low and semi-circular while the fourth on the north face rose several storeys above the wall and acted as a watchtower. Within the enclosure was the small but luxurious accommodation for himself and his family. Two hundred white marble steps led up to the summit where a drawbridge gave access to the interior. The superstructure has disappeared over the years so all that can now be seen from the outside is the conical earthwork.

At the base of the mountain he constructed a separate palace for the reception of his guests. Nearby a large artificial pool was created with a circular pavilion in the centre. This had the dual purpose of serving as a reservoir for the water which was channelled into it from a source near Bethlehem, as well as providing an attractive place for swimming and relaxation. The area was surrounded by a formal garden. The Jewish historian Flavius Josephus records that Agrippa, son-in-law of the Emperor Augustus, stayed in the palace as a guest of Herod in 15 BC. He also records that Herod died at Jericho and gives a detailed account of his funeral cortege on its way to the Herodion, but in spite of extensive excavations since 1962 no trace of his tomb has been found.

In AD 70, during the First Jewish Revolt against the Romans, the fortress was used as a refuge by the insurgents. Later, in the Second Revolt from 132–135, the Zealot leader Bar Kokhba developed the fortress as his headquarters. The Herodion water cisterns were extended to form a complicated underground network of tunnels from which surprise attacks could be made. A synagogue and 'mikve' (ritual cleansing bath) were also constructed within the walls.

After the defeat of the Zealots, the Herodion remained unoccupied for some three hundred years. Between the fifth and the seventh centuries monks, possibly of Egyptian origin, inhabited the site and there are many Christian symbols on the walls. A chapel was built amongst the remains at the top, and another at the foot of the mountain. There is no evidence of any particular habitation after the seventh century.

Tour

The approach is via a modern road at the foot of the mountain, passing beside the remains of the Herodion pool which is partially flanked by re-erected pillars. A better idea of the extensive layout can be gained from the top of the mountain which is over 350ft higher than its surroundings. Halfway up are a car park, toilets, and a ticket booth. From here there is a fairly steep 200 metre path to the top including 55 shallow steps.

At the summit the impression is of standing on the rim of a volcano whose crater surprisingly contains the remains of a compact royal residence. The foundations of the original entrance to the fortress which was approached by two hundred marble steps, can be seen below the modern footbridge on the left. Looking down into the palace ruins, and also on the left, is the base of the large circular watchtower. Immediately in front of it can be seen the extent of Herod's colonnaded courtyard.

Walk round to the right passing the foundations of the northern semi-circular defensive tower and proceed to a position between the head of the stairway leading down into the interior and the foundations of the western defensive tower. From here other features of the site are identifiable. Immediately below are the remains of the 5th/7th century chapel built within part of Herod's residential accommodation. To the left of the foot of the stairway, and immediately below the northern tower, are the remains of his bath-house in typical Roman layout. The roofed complex was subsequently occupied by the monks who utilised Herod's caldarium (hot room) as a bakery. On the extreme right of the ruins is a rectangular area, originally the dining hall, which was later adapted by the Zealots for use as a synagogue. They added the stone slab seating on three sides.

Before descending the steps enjoy the panoramic views of the Judaean hills and the wilderness beyond. To the north-west in the far distance can be seen the taller buildings of Jerusalem, while much nearer lies Bethlehem. If time permits make a closer inspection of the ruins the main features of which are clearly marked. The entrance to the Bar Kokhba underground defence network is reached via a stairway in the corner of the colonnaded courtyard. If the door is locked the key may be obtained from the ticket office.

On the way down to the car park (either from the top or the exit from the Bar Kokhba tunnels) there are good views of part of the lower palace complex at the foot of the mountain. The outline of the rectangular pool with its circular central feature is very clear as is the surrounding levelled area where Herod laid out his formal garden. Excavations between the garden and the mountain foot have revealed another building, the purpose of which has not been established.

Opening Times:
April to September: 8.00–17.00
October to March: 8.00–16.00
On eve of Shabbat and holidays closes 1 hour earlier. Closed on Yom Kippur. The tourist 'green card' is accepted.

Souvenir Shop: Only a few postcards at the ticket office

Toilets: Beside the car park

Custodian:
The National Parks Authority

Bethany

Bethany was a 'home from home' for the Galileans and it was here that Jesus often stayed when visiting Jerusalem. A modern Franciscan Church has been built over the traditional home of Lazarus, Martha and Mary. There is a Mosque above the reputed tomb where Jesus raised Lazarus from the dead. Close to a modern Greek Orthodox Church can be seen the ruins of a Crusader tower. Simon the Leper also lived in the village, although the site of his home has not been identified.

Access

1. *By Car:* The straggling village is on the Jericho Road about 4 km from Jerusalem. The slender bell tower and the cupola of the Franciscan Church can be seen on the left of the road at the end of the second double-bend.

Here there is a bus stop and a small parking space. The site may be reached either by going through a gate leading into a walled garden between the road and the Church or, by following the wall round keeping to the left and walking up the narrow road.

2. *On foot:* It is possible to walk from Jerusalem via the top of the Mount of Olives (please refer to the map on page 4). From the top of Olivet take the road running east between the high walls and then fork right. After a short distance there is a magnificent view of the village of Bethphage and Upper Bethany with the Judaean Wilderness beyond. On a clear day it is possible to see the Mountains of Moab the other side of the Jordan Valley. Walk down the road to the walled Franciscan Monastery which marks the place where 'the two ways meet'. (See details of this Church under 'Bethphage'.) Follow the boundary walls round on the right hand side and on to the ancient track leading down to Bethany. Continue southwards and be sure to keep straight ahead at the cross roads. The village will eventually come into view. The track is very steep and one should allow at least 45 minutes from the top of the Mount of Olives.

* * *

THE FRANCISCAN CHURCH

The building was completed in 1954 and is dedicated to St Lazarus. It stands among the ruins of three earlier churches. The Italian Architect Barluzzi, who always tried to make his buildings expressive of the events they

The Anointing of Jesus by Mary (John 12. 1–8)

Six days before the Passover festival Jesus came to Bethany, the home of Lazarus whom he had raised from the dead. They gave a supper in his honour, at which Martha served, and Lazarus was among the guests with Jesus. Then Mary brought a pound of very costly perfume, pure oil of nard, and anointed Jesus's feet and wiped them with her hair, till the house was filled with the fragrance.

At this, Judas Iscariot, one of his disciples – the one who was to betray him – protested, 'Could not this perfume have been sold for three hundred denarii and the money given to the poor?' He said this, not out of any concern for the poor, but because he was a thief; he had charge of the common purse and used to pilfer the money kept in it. 'Leave her alone,' said Jesus. 'Let her keep it for the day of my burial. The poor you have always among you, but you will not always have me.' (REB)

'Take my love; my Lord, I pour
at thy feet its treasure-store;
take myself, and I will be
ever, only, all for thee.'

For further Gospel references, see page 195

commemorate, has contrasted the rather dark interior, resembling a mausoleum, with the light flooding from the dome reminding Christians of the Resurrection. The earliest Church was erected in the middle of the fourth century soon after the Emperor Constantine built his great Basilicas in Bethlehem and Jerusalem. Some of the lower courses of masonry among the ruins surrounding the modern Church date from this period.

The first Church was damaged by an earthquake but was replaced by a larger one in the 5th/6th century. This was destroyed by the Persians in AD 614. Some fine mosaics from these two Byzantine churches can be seen a few inches below the level of the courtyard in front of the Church and also incorporated in the floor to the right of the nave.

In the twelfth century the Crusaders built a very large Benedictine Convent encompassing the whole area of the earlier churches, the Tomb of Lazarus further along the road, and stretching as far as the modern Greek Orthodox Church. The tower, now in ruins, marked the western boundary of the Convent.

Tour

The present Church is designed in the form of a Greek cross. Notice inside, the mosaics high up on the four walls: On the left Jesus is depicted with Martha and Mary; above the main altar the theme is 'I am the Resurrection and the Life'; on the right Jesus raises Lazarus from the dead; and above the entrance door Jesus dines with Simon the Leper.

Around the cupola is an inscription in Latin from John 11.25: 'He that believeth in me, though he were dead, yet shall he live: and whosoever liveth and believeth in me shall never die'. Portrayed in the mosaics of the dome are blossoms, with flames and doves symbolising faithful souls which take flight to heaven.

On leaving the Church walk diagonally across to the far left corner of the courtyard and mount the steps to see into a building open to the skies where a roof arch stands aloft over these ancient walls. The stones on the left were part of the Crusader Benedictine Convent, whilst those at the end and on the right are Byzantine and date from the 5th/6th century.

On the left there are a series of rooms which were once part of the Convent. In one long room is a millstone together with an ancient deeply cut wooden screw which was part of an olive press. The largest of the rooms has been converted for use as a chapel.

THE TOMB OF LAZARUS

Leave the Church courtyard and walk further up the road where, on the left, is the reputed Tomb of Lazarus. Entry is by way of 26 steps down a steep shaft. At the bottom, a further three shallow steps connect the vestibule with the inner chamber and it is necessary to crouch low under a stone slab in order to enter the tomb. According to tradition, it was in the vestibule that Jesus stood when he called Lazarus from the dead. The tomb is lined with ancient stone blocks for protection.

In the fourth century there was a Byzantine shrine over the site. During the Crusader period the entrance to the tomb was from within the Benedictine Convent and after this was destroyed, access was from the Mosque which is now above it. The Muslims also venerate St Lazarus. The present steps leading from the road were constructed by them in the sixteenth century.

On leaving the tomb, walk further up the road where, on the left, is the modern Greek Orthodox Church dedicated to Simon the Leper and completed in 1964. Behind it can clearly be seen the ruins of the west tower of the twelfth century Benedictine Convent. This was built upon much earlier foundations and it is interesting to note that the base contains some massive Herodian stone blocks. To follow the traditional 'Palm Sunday Walk', turn right at the junction by the Church.

Authors' Comments

Many guided tours allow insufficient time at Bethany using it only as a short break in a long day visiting Jericho, the Dead Sea and Masada. The village deserves much more attention because it was a favoured resting place of Jesus and as such is referred to a number of times in each of the four gospels. More importantly it was here that in calling forth Lazarus from the tomb, Our Lord demonstrated so vividly his power to raise the dead.

Opening Times:
Franciscan Church
8.00–11.25 14.00–17.00 daily
(Winter closes 16.30)
Tomb of Lazarus Admission on request at the shop opposite. A small fee is charged

Souvenir Shop:
Opposite the Tomb of Lazarus
Refreshments available

Toilets: At the far end of the Church courtyard. Also to the left of the Souvenir shop

Custodians:
The Church The Franciscans
The Tomb The Muslims

Telephone:
The Church (02) 749291

Bethphage

The Franciscan Monastery stands within high walls at a place where 'the two ways meet'. According to tradition it was here that Jesus mounted the donkey to make his triumphal entry into Jerusalem on the first Palm Sunday.

Access

By car or on foot: From Gethsemane follow the instructions to reach the Place of the Ascension (*see page 5*), but continue on past the shrine for about 100 metres until reaching the wall ahead surrounding the Church of Pater Noster. Here turn left. Continue eastward between the high walls and take the right fork. After a short distance there is a magnificent view of the village of Bethphage and Upper Bethany with the Judaean Wilderness beyond. On a clear day it is possible to see the Mountains of Moab the other side of the Jordan Valley. Proceed down the road and straight ahead is the walled Franciscan Monastery.

Allow twelve minutes walking from the top of Olivet.

Details

The Monastery was built in 1883 on a twelfth century Crusader site. Ring the bell for admission, and once inside walk across the courtyard to the Church. On the left of the nave, protected by a wrought iron grille, is an ancient stone cube measuring about a metre square. There is a tradition that Our Lord mounted the donkey from this stone. The early paintings on each face were restored in 1950. They portray: on the north side, the Disciples collecting the donkey; on the east, the crowd receiving palms; on the south, Jesus calling Lazarus from the tomb; and on the west, Jesus with Martha and Mary.

Above the altar is a mural of Jesus riding on the donkey and receiving the acclaim of the crowds. Around the walls are scenes from the Palm Sunday story, whilst the ceiling of the Church is attractively painted with tiny sprays of flowers.

It is worthwhile seeking permission to visit the first century tombs in the olive grove at the rear of the monastery. If this is granted, descend the path and on the right hand side is a fine example of a tomb with its rolling stone still intact. There are a number of other burial chambers in the vicinity and it is here that the Galileans who died whilst visiting Jerusalem were laid to rest.

Opening Times:
7.00–11.45 14.00–17.30 daily
(Winter: closes at 16.30)
Ring the bell

Souvenir Shop: None

Toilets: To the right of the entrance courtyard

Custodian: The Franciscans. The gatekeeper appreciates a small gratuity

Telephone: (02) 284352

The Triumphal Entry into Jerusalem (Mark 11. 1–10)

They were now approaching Jerusalem, and when they reached Bethphage and Bethany, close by the Mount of Olives, Jesus sent off two of his disciples. 'Go into the village opposite,' he told them, 'and just as you enter you will find tethered there a colt which no one has yet ridden. Untie it and bring it here. If anyone asks why you are doing this, say, "The Master needs it, and will send it back here without delay."' So they went off, and found the colt outside in the street, tethered beside a door. As they were untying it, some of the bystanders asked, 'What are you doing, untying that colt?' They answered as Jesus had told them, and were then allowed to take it. So they brought the colt to Jesus, and when they had spread their cloaks on it he mounted it. Many people carpeted the road with their cloaks, while others spread greenery which they had cut in the fields; and those in front and those behind shouted, 'Hosanna! Blessed is he who comes in the name of the Lord! Blessed is the kingdom of our father David which is coming! Hosanna in the heavens!' (REB)

'The people of the Hebrews
with palms before thee went:
our praise and prayer and anthems
before thee we present.'

For further Gospel references, see page 195

Ein Kerim

Church of the Visitation
Church of St John the Baptist

A pleasant village about seven kilometres west of Jerusalem, the traditional home of the priest Zechariah and his wife Elizabeth. The Virgin Mary visited her cousin here, and it was the birthplace and home of St John the Baptist.

Access

By car: From the north west corner of the Old City take the main Tel-Aviv Road named Jaffa Street. In about 2 km turn left at the junction and in ½ km bear left into the Herzl Boulevard. Continue along this main thoroughfare for a further 2 km until reaching the Military Cemetery and Herzl Memorial Park on the right. (Behind this is Yad Vashem.) Turn right at the traffic lights by a modern steel sculpture. This road leads down to the village which is about 2 km further on. Parking space is available on the left opposite the village Police Station.

THE CHURCH OF THE VISITATION

Access

From the centre of the village the Church is reached by walking down the road to the left. In about 300 metres, notice the old village spring which has the minaret of a mosque above it. The spring is interesting because here is a natural water source which must have been familiar to the Virgin Mary when she stayed

in this 'hill country of Judaea' with her cousin Elizabeth. Walk along the path opposite. The Church will be reached in another 450 metres, but be careful to keep to the right in order to avoid taking an alternative track which leads up to the Convent of the Russian White Sisters. Further along climb the steep slope and series of steps to the Church.

Tour

First notice the fine wrought-iron screen at the entrance to the courtyard. Then look at

the mosaic on the west facade of the Church depicting the Blessed Virgin Mary, mounted on a donkey, meeting her cousin Elizabeth. The Church, completed in 1955, was erected over the remains of earlier Byzantine and Crusader buildings.

Proceed to the Lower Chapel by walking through the cloister arches directly below the mosaic. This area dates from the sixth century. Standing at the entrance notice ahead a tunnel leading to an old well. There is an ancient tradition that the waters joyfully sprang out of the rock here when the Virgin Mary greeted her cousin. The three large paintings on the walls of the Chapel portray: Zechariah performing his priestly duties in the Temple; The Visitation; and the

---

The Visitation of Mary to Elizabeth (Luke 1. 39–56)

And Mary arose in those days, and went into the hill country with haste, into a city of Judah; and entered into the house of Zacharias, and saluted Elisabeth. And it came to pass, that when Elisabeth heard the salutation of Mary, the babe leaped in her womb; and Elisabeth was filled with the Holy Ghost: And she spake out with a loud voice, and said, 'Blessed art thou among women, and blessed is the fruit of thy womb. And whence is this to me, that the mother of my Lord should come to me? For lo, as soon as the voice of thy salutation sounded in mine ears, the babe leaped in my womb for joy. And blessed is she that believed: for there shall be a performance of those things which were told her from the Lord'.

And Mary said, 'My soul doth magnify the Lord, and my spirit hath rejoiced in God my Saviour. For he hath regarded the low estate of his handmaiden: for, behold, from henceforth all generations shall call me blessed. For he that is mighty hath done to me great things; and holy is his name. And his mercy is on them that fear him, from generation to generation. He hath shewed strength with his arm; he hath scattered the proud in the imagination of their hearts. He hath put down the mighty from their seats, and exalted them of low degree. He hath filled the hungry with good things, and the rich he hath sent empty away. He hath holpen his servant Israel, in remembrance of his mercy; as he spake to our fathers, to Abraham, and to his seed for ever'. And Mary abode with her about three months, and returned to her own house. (AV)

'Still to the lowly soul
he doth himself impart,
and for his dwelling and his throne
chooseth the pure in heart.'

---

slaughtering of the innocent babes by King Herod's soldiers. Below this is a rock set in a niche known as the Stone of Hiding which, according to the second century 'Testimony of James', is reputed to have concealed St John the Baptist from the perils of the sword.

After leaving the Chapel, cross the courtyard to examine the attractive ceramic plaques on the wall opposite. The words spoken by the Blessed Virgin, more familiar as The Magnificat, are displayed here in 45 different languages.

In order to reach the Upper Church, ascend the steps to the left of the cloister arches. The interior is decorated with paintings depicting the glorification of the Virgin through the centuries, and also Holy Women of the Old and New Testaments. Notice the large stone blocks in the wall of the apse which formed part of the Crusader church. Some of the paintings above illustrate incidents from the life of Mary, whilst the one in the centre depicts the dedication of the building by the Roman Catholic Patriarch and the Custos of the Holy Land.

Five large paintings adorn the south wall. Looking at them from the apse these portray: the Council of Ephesus when the Blessed Virgin was proclaimed the Mother of God; the protection of the Church by Mary; the miracle of turning the water into wine at Cana in Galilee; the Battle of Lepoto which was won through the intercession of Mary; and on the far right John Duns Scotus defending the Immaculate Conception before the Sorbonne. The mosaic floor of the Church is particularly attractive and depicts natures tribute to Mary.

Before returning to the village, pause outside the wrought-iron screen to look down upon Ein Kerim which is dominated by the spire of the Church of the Nativity of St John the Baptist. Notice how the buildings of modern Jerusalem are just beginning to encroach into this area. Nevertheless, the view across these Judaean hills is still comparatively unspoilt and delightfully rural.

Authors' Comments

The Church of the Visitation is probably one of the most beautiful of all the Gospel sites in the Holy Land. This peaceful setting is an excellent place for meditation.

Opening Times:
8.00–11.45 14.30–18.00
Winter closes at 17.00
Closed on Saturday

Souvenir Shop: Sometimes open

Toilets: In the courtyard

Custodian: The Franciscans

Telephone: (02) 417291

THE CHURCH OF
ST JOHN THE BAPTIST

Access

From the centre of the village
the Church is reached by
walking up the road to the
right for about 100 metres
passing through an archway.

Tour

The facade has a fortress-like
appearance although it was
rebuilt as recently as the
seventeenth century on the
lines of an earlier Crusader
building. However, remnants
of two chapels belonging to a
fifth century church have been

found under the substantial
west porch of the present
structure.

From the courtyard ascend
the steps to reach this porch
and enter the Church. The
interior is rather dark and it
takes some time to adjust to
the dim light. Of particular
interest is a high dado of blue
and white tiles on the massive
central pillars and walls.
These were brought from
Valencia in Spain. A large
Crusader mosaic has been
relaid in the centre of the nave
and another under the dome.

The main feature of the
Church is the grotto of the
Benedictus which is reputed

The Birth and Naming of John the Baptist (Luke 1. 57–66)

*When the time came for Elizabeth's child to be born, she gave birth to a
son. Her neighbours and relatives heard what great kindness the Lord
had shown to her, and they shared her delight. On the eighth day they
came to circumcise the child; and they were going to name him Zechariah
after his father, but his mother spoke up: 'No!' she said. 'He is to be called
John.' 'But', they said, 'there is nobody in your family who has that
name'. They enquired of his father by signs what he would like him to be
called. He asked for a writing tablet and to everybody's astonishment
wrote, 'His name is John.' Immediately his lips and tongue were freed
and he began to speak, praising God. All the neighbours were overcome
with awe, and throughout the uplands of Judaea the whole story became
common talk. All who heard it were deeply impressed and said, 'What
will this child become?' For indeed the hand of the Lord was upon him.*
(REB)

'The great forerunner of the morn,
The herald of the Word, is born;
And faithful hearts shall never fail
With thanks and praise his light to hail.'

For further Gospel references, see page 196

to be part of the home of Zechariah and Elizabeth and thus the birthplace of St John the Baptist. To reach it descend the flight of steps at the east end of the north aisle. The floor and the apse date from the twelfth century. The traditional place of birth is marked by a medallion under the altar.

Authors' Comments

The site dates from the fifth century and is the only one to be reverenced as the birthplace of St John the Baptist.

Opening Times:
Summer: 8.00–12.00 14.30–18.00 (Winter closes 17.00)
Closed on Saturday
Sundays: 9.00–12.00 14.30–17.00

Souvenir Shop: To the right of the entrance portico

Toilets: None

Custodian: The Franciscans

Telephone: (02) 413639

Emmaus

St Luke records that, on the day of his Resurrection, Jesus joined two disciples as they journeyed on the road to the village of Emmaus about seven miles from Jerusalem. At first they thought he was a stranger and did not recognise him. When they reached their destination, they persuaded him to stay with them and it was there during the meal that he revealed himself in the breaking of bread. The location of the Gospel Emmaus is unknown but over the years four possible sites have been suggested.

AMWAS

Here within a walled compound, are the extensive ruins of a substantial fifth century Byzantine Church and some evidence of later Crusader occupation. Unfortunately the entrance gate is often locked and it is then only possible to view the ruins from a distance.

Access

Sometimes known today as Latrun, about 26 km (19 miles) from Jerusalem off the main Tel-Aviv highway. When the coastal plain comes into view, take the first turning on the right to Ramallah at the Latrun junction. The site is almost immediately on the right behind an iron gate but can be missed because the ruins are not easily visible from the road.

Details

This site is the oldest of the three. It was mentioned several times by the historian Josephus in the first century, and later by both St Jerome and Eusebius in the fourth century when the town had the Roman name of Nicopolis. The first church here was built in the fifth century, but like so many others in the land, was vandalised by the Persians after AD 614. The name Amwas is an Arab corruption of the word Emmaus (hot spring).

In the twelfth century the Crusaders erected a smaller church within the nave of the Byzantine Basilica. Today the ruins are deserted but are most impressive and the three Byzantine apses still rise to a height of about twenty feet. There are a number of floor-mosaics which, sadly, are rapidly deteriorating. The Byzantine baptismal place to the north of the ruins is particularly interesting because the ceremony involved total immersion by the priest who stood in a higher section where only his feet were in the water.

During the Crusader period doubts were cast as to the validity of the site when greater credence was given to the earlier manuscripts of St Luke. These gave the distance of Emmaus from Jerusalem as only 60 stadia (7 miles). In later transcriptions 160 stadia (19 miles) was mentioned, but many considered that it was unlikely that the two disciples would have walked the 38 mile double journey in the same day. Alternative sites 60 stadia from Jerusalem were

therefore sought and apparently two were chosen: Abu Gosh and El Qubeibah.

* * *

ABU GOSH

A well preserved Crusader Church in a tranquil setting adjoining a Benedictine Monastery.

Access

The village is also off the main highway to Tel-Aviv about 11 km (7 miles) from Jerusalem. From the large roundabout (connecting the northern ring-road and other main roads in the north-west of the modern City) drive towards Tel-Aviv and in 6½ km pass under a road bridge. In a further 2 km bear off to the right, signposted Qiryat Yearim. In 2½ km take the turning on the left towards the Benedictine Monastery which is situated in a cluster of trees. The high walls of its compound are clearly visible as is the minaret of a nearby

mosque. Ring the bell for admission.

Details

Within the peaceful grounds and adjoining the monastery is an impressive Crusader church very similar to that of St Anne's in Jerusalem. In the crypt is a spring dating from neolithic times which was used by the Roman Tenth Legion when they camped here in AD 70. An original plaque commemorating the event has been inserted in the wall to the left of the door leading into the crypt.

Throughout the middle ages the building was used as a hostelry. At the beginning of the nineteenth century the brigand, Abu Gosh, after whom the village has now been named, robbed travellers as they journeyed from the coast to Jerusalem. Those who refused to pay found themselves prisoners here.

After the Crimean War, the Turkish Sultan presented the ruins to Napoleon III who in turn entrusted them to the French Benedictine Lazarus Fathers. Restoration was carried out at the beginning of this century. Since 1976 the monastery has been occupied by monks and nuns from the Benedictine Community in Bec, Normandy. The Church is dedicated to The Resurrection and is a most suitable place in which to recall Our Lord's appearance to the two disciples.

Towering above the village can be seen a huge statue of the Madonna and Child surmounting the Church of Our Lady of the Ark of the Covenant. The building was constructed in the 1920s on the foundations of a Byzantine church and commemorates the fact that the Ark rested here for twenty years before being taken by King David to Jerusalem, circa 1000 BC.

Opening Times: 8.30–11.00 14.30–17.00 Closed Sundays and Thursdays

Souvenir Shop: To the left of the main building

Toilets: Beside the souvenir shop

Custodian: The Benedictines

Telephone: (02) 342798

*   *   *

EL QUBEIBAH

The present twentieth century church follows the line of an earlier one constructed by the Crusaders. Within the grounds is a section of Roman road believed by the Franciscans to be the one mentioned in the Gospel narrative.

Access

Like Abu Gosh, the site is also approximately 11 km (7 miles) from Jerusalem. Join the main highway between the Damascus and New Gates by the palm plantation. After leaving the traffic lights by the palms, keep straight ahead through the next two sets of

lights and turn left at the third (signposted Ramot Alon) into Shemuel Ha'navi Street. Keep on this route for 7½ km to the highest point. On the right at the top of the hill and surmounted by a minaret, is Nabi Samwil, the traditional site of the tomb of the Prophet Samuel. Shortly afterwards, and before descending the hill, turn left into an unmarked road which leads into the arab village of El Qubeibah. At a junction in the centre of the village keep straight ahead and in a further kilometre the compound is on the right behind a stone wall.

Tour

A peaceful location standing 800 metres above sea level from which there are fine views across the surrounding countryside. Within the compound a section of Roman road has been excavated. It is claimed that this was part of the route which linked Jerusalem with Caesarea and that the two disciples walked along it with the risen Jesus on the first Easter Day.

The Church, dedicated to the one named Cleopas, was consecrated in 1902. It is built upon the line of an earlier Crusader church the foundations of which are visible in the lower courses of the sanctuary. To the left of the nave, protected by a glass and wood panel in the floor, are the remains of what is claimed to be the house of Cleopas.

On Easter Monday there is a large public pilgrimage to El Qubeibah when the Franciscan 'Custodian' of the Holy Land blesses the bread.

Opening Times:
8.00–11.45 14.00–18.00 daily
(Winter closes 17.00)
Ring the bell

Shop: None

Toilets: In the garden

Custodian: The Franciscans

Telephone: (02) 952495 (Ext 4)

Resurrection Appearance on the Road to Emmaus
(Luke 24. 13–35)

That same day two of the disciples were on their way to a village called Emmaus, about seven miles from Jerusalem, talking together about all that had happened. As they talked and argued, Jesus himself came up and walked with them; but something prevented them from recognizing him.

He asked them, 'What is it you are debating as you walk?' They stood still, their faces full of sadness, and one, called Cleopas, answered, 'Are you the only person staying in Jerusalem not to have heard the news of what has happened there in the last few days?' 'What news?' he said. 'About Jesus of Nazareth,' they replied, 'who, by deeds and words of power, proved himself a prophet in the sight of God and the whole people; and how our chief priests and rulers handed him over to be sentenced to death, and crucified him. But we had been hoping that he was to be the liberator of Israel. What is more, this is the third day since it happened, and now some women of our company have astounded us: they went early to the tomb, but failed to find his body, and returned with a story that they had seen a vision of angels who told them he was alive. Then some of our people went to the tomb and found things just as the women had said; but him they did not see.'

'How dull you are!' he answered. 'How slow to believe all that the prophets said! Was not the Messiah bound to suffer in this way before entering upon his glory?' Then, starting from Moses and all the prophets, he explained to them in the whole of scripture the things that referred to himself.

By this time they had reached the village to which they were going, and he made as if to continue his journey. But they pressed him: 'Stay with us, for evening approaches, and the day is almost over.' So he went in to stay with them. And when he had sat down with them at table, he took bread and said the blessing; he broke the bread and offered it to them. Then their eyes were opened, and they recognized him; but he vanished from their sight. They said one to another, 'Were not our hearts on fire as he talked with us on the road and explained the scriptures to us?'

Without a moment's delay they set out and returned to Jerusalem. There they found that the eleven and the rest of the company had assembled, and were saying, 'It is true: the Lord has risen; he has appeared to Simon.' Then they described what had happened on their journey and told how he had made himself known to them in the breaking of the bread. (REB)

> 'He is risen, he is risen!
> Tell it with a joyful voice;
> He has burst his three days' prison;
> Let the whole wide earth rejoice.'

For further Gospel references, see page 196

QALUNIEH

This fourth possible site of Emmaus is only mentioned here because it appears in a number of guide books and therefore requires an explanation.

The Arab village 6.5 km (4 miles) from Jerusalem, earlier known as Colonia, was totally destroyed in 1948. It was situated just off the modern highway to Tel-Aviv. Josephus mentions this other 'Emmaous' as a refuge for 800 veterans of the Jewish–Roman War after the sacking of Jerusalem by Titus in AD 70. The only factor in its favour is that it was sufficiently near the City for the two disciples to have made the journey there and back comfortably in the same day. Modern houses have been built on the site of the old village and there is now nothing to view.

Jericho

The word Jericho means 'City of Palms', aptly named because of its setting in a green fertile oasis at the lowest inhabited place on earth 1,300 feet (394 metres) below sea level. Here Jesus healed Bartimaeus, the blind beggar, and dined with Zacchaeus, the rich tax collector, who had climbed a sycamore tree to gain a better view of him. Our Lord also chose the road to Jericho as the setting for his Parable of the Good Samaritan. He was undoubtedly very familiar with the area as he must often have passed through it when taking the route from Galilee to Jerusalem along the Jordan Valley.

Access from Jerusalem

A distance of 41 km along the main road. From the north-east corner of the Old City follow the Jericho Road passing the Garden of Gethsemane; continue on through Bethany and into the open country. Shortly afterwards a modern highway joins the road from the left. The Inn of the Good Samaritan will be reached in about 8 km from here. It lies on the right at the top of a fairly steep ascent.

THE INN OF THE GOOD SAMARITAN

It should be remembered that Jesus merely used an inn as part of the setting for his Parable of the Good Samaritan which he told in

114

response to the question: 'Who is my neighbour?'. It seems likely however that there has been some sort of travellers' rest at this point for thousands of years, bearing in mind that Jericho itself is the oldest known inhabited place on earth and travellers to Jerusalem coming up from the Jordan Valley would have gained their first view of the Mount of Olives and Mount Scopus from here. There is ample evidence of earlier buildings on either side of the road.

In 1903 the Turks constructed a Police Post on the traditional site of the Inn, but this was partially destroyed by the British in 1917. In more recent times the ruins have been converted into an Israeli gift shop.

Access (continued)

Drive on for about 3½ km and look out for a turning off to the left signposted Nahal Perat. Here a decision has to be made as to whether to continue along the main road, or take the turning to pick up the very narrow and twisting Wadi Kelt road.

Route 1. *The Main Road* Proceed for a further 4 km and look out on the right for a fairly large stone inscribed 'Sea Level'. In the tourist season there is often an

---

The Parable of the Good Samaritan (Luke 10. 30–37)

Jesus replied, 'A man was on his way from Jerusalem down to Jericho when he was set upon by robbers, who stripped and beat him, and went off leaving him half dead. It so happened that a priest was going down by the same road, and when he saw him, he went past on the other side. So too a Levite came to the place, and when he saw him went past on the other side. But a Samaritan who was going that way came upon him, and when he saw him he was moved to pity. He went up and bandaged his wounds, bathing them with oil and wine. Then he lifted him on to his own beast, brought him to an inn, and looked after him.

Next day he produced two silver pieces and gave them to the innkeeper, and said, "Look after him; and if you spend more, I will repay you on my way back." Which of these three do you think was neighbour to the man who fell into the hands of the robbers?' He answered, 'The one who showed him kindness.' Jesus said to him, 'Go and do as he did.' (REB)

'When I needed a neighbour, were you there,
were you there?
And the creed and the colour and the name won't matter,
were you there?'

---

enterprising Bedouin near it with his camel to attract photographers.

Shortly after this the Jordan Valley and the Dead Sea come into view. In the distance can be seen the Mountains of Moab, and Mount Nebo from where Moses, having led the tribes of Israel out of Egypt, had a view of the Promised Land before his death. On entering the valley look out for the first turning on the left which leads to Jericho. The distance from here to the town is about 8 km.

Route 2. *Via the Wadi Kelt Road*

Turn left off the main Jericho Road, then almost immediately turn left again and continue until reaching another road rising sharply back to the right. Take this road which becomes very narrow and twisting with little room in places to pass another car. In about 4 km there is a small parking space on the left with a cross on the hill above it. From the cross there is a view of St George's Monastery which literally clings to the ravine edge on the other side of the Wadi Kelt Valley.

The Monastery was founded in AD 480 by John of Thebes who for a time became Bishop of Caesarea. St George of Koziba lived here in the sixth century and subsequently the foundation was named after him. Much of the present building dates from Crusader times and was restored by the Greek Orthodox Church towards the end of the nineteenth century.

Continue along the twisting road from which later on there are fine views of the Jericho oasis. A little further along still, notice on the left that the Wadi Kelt runs parallel to the road and eventually crosses it. At this point there is a good view across the valley to the archaeological excavations of Herod's Palace and the first century town around it. This is known as 'New Testament Jericho' although it seems likely that the present town, within the oasis, was also inhabited in Our Lord's time.

Descend into the Jordan Valley. The main road will be joined near a Police Station on the outskirts of the town.

JERICHO TOWN

No Church has yet been built to specifically commemorate either of the two Gospel events which took place here. However, there are Roman Catholic and Greek Orthodox churches which serve the local population. It is a very untidy and scruffy town, although prior to 1948 there were some fine houses belonging to wealthy Palestinians. In the centre can be seen a large sycamore tree reminiscent of the one Zacchaeus climbed to have a better view of Jesus.

Old Testament Jericho (Tel Es-Sultan)

The earliest known inhabited place on earth is situated about 2 km north of the modern town, to the left of the main road leading up the Jordan Valley. The word 'Tel' is the name for an ancient mound formed through the centuries as the result of a city being razed to the ground many times, and on each occasion rebuilt on top of the rubble. In this instance evidence of over 21 previous civilisations has been unearthed and at its highest point the mound is 45 feet (15 metres) above the road.

Considering its antiquity and importance, the first view of the Tel from the road is not particularly impressive and the total area is surprisingly small, only five acres. The first inhabitants settled here about 10,000 years ago, but the site has not been occupied since the Babylonian exile. It had therefore already been in a state of ruin for over 500 years before the birth of Christ.

The outstanding feature is a substantial watchtower which was uncovered in a deep trench cut by the British Archaeologist, the late Dr Kathleen Kenyon, in the

---

The Story of Zacchaeus (Luke 19. 1–10)

Entering Jericho Jesus made his way through the city. There was a man there named Zacchaeus; he was superintendent of taxes and very rich. He was eager to see what Jesus looked like; but, being a little man, he could not see him for the crowd. So he ran on ahead and climbed a sycamore tree in order to see him, for he was to pass that way.

When Jesus came to the place, he looked up and said, 'Zacchaeus, be quick and come down, for I must stay at your house today.' He climbed down as quickly as he could and welcomed him gladly. At this there was a general murmur of disapproval. 'He has gone in to be the guest of a sinner,' they said. But Zacchaeus stood there and said to the Lord, 'Here and now, sir, I give half of my possessions to charity; and if I have defrauded anyone, I will repay him four times over.' Jesus said to him, 'Today salvation has come to this house – for this man too is a son of Abraham. The Son of Man has come to seek and to save what is lost.' (REB)

'Blest be the Lord, who comes to men
With messages of grace;
Who comes, in God his Father's name,
To save our sinful race.'

For further Gospel references, see page 197

mid-1950s. This stands as a monument to the incredible achievements of an unknown Stone Age people who lived here around 8000 BC. Even more remarkable is the fact that within the tower there is still a perfectly formed staircase.

At some points towards the perimeter of the Tel can be seen the remnants of the ancient mud-brick walls similar in style to those made famous by the story recorded in Joshua 6.1–21. At the blowing of the trumpets the walls came tumbling down.

Looking westwards from the Tel notice the Greek Orthodox Monastery of the Temptation which clings to the cliff edge in a similar way to that of St George's Monastery in the Wadi Kelt Valley.

At the foot of the Tel, on the other side of the road, is a water source known as Elisha's Spring which not only supplied the early inhabitants, but has been one of the main sources of irrigation for the fertile oasis for thousands of years. Pumping gear has now been installed and consequently it is not possible to view the spring itself.

Opening Times:
The Tel:
April to September: 8.00–17.00
Fridays: 8.00–16.00
October to March: 8.00–16.00
Fridays: 9.00–15.00
Closed on Yom Kippur
The tourist 'Green Card' is accepted

Souvenir Shop: None

Toilets: Inside the entrance on either side

Custodian: The National Parks Authority

Telephone: (02) 922909

Masada

The Masada story must surely be one of the most dramatic and moving in the history of mankind. Here in AD 73 on this table-top mountain overlooking the Dead Sea, 960 men, women and children, having withstood a prolonged siege, chose to die by their own swords rather than submit to Roman slavery.

Access

Masada lies to the south of Jerusalem about 110 km by road via the western shore of the Dead Sea. Allow about two hours. Follow the access instructions for Qumran on page 129 as far as the 'bus stop where there is a turning off to the right, signposted Qumran'. From here continue south on the main road for 36 km to pass through the oasis of En Gedi where there is a public bathing beach. About 14 km further on start looking out on the right for the rocky mass of Masada. When almost opposite the mountain turn off onto the approach road by a bus stop. After 4 km there is a large coach and car park. The top of Masada is reached by cable car in two and a half minutes, or for the very fit via the 'Snake Path'. Allow at least forty minutes for the steep climb.

If ascending by cable-car, visitors should be warned that on leaving the terminal at the top it is necessary to climb an external wooden stairway to reach the admission booth. There are sixty-six fairly shallow steps but the ground below can be seen between each one.

The price of the cable-car ticket normally includes admission to the site. However visitors in possession of the National Parks Authority tourist 'green card' need only pay for the cable-car.

History

Flavius Josephus the first-century AD historian, in his

book 'Jewish War', provides a detailed record of the sequence of events which occurred here. Around the end of the first century BC Alexander Jannaeus built a fortress on the summit. Later in 40 BC the young Herod was forced to leave Jerusalem and used Masada as a safe refuge for his family. He left them with a garrison of 800 men whilst he made his way to Rome where he was nominated King of Judaea by Mark Anthony. While he was away Masada proved its value as a stronghold capable of withstanding siege. Being encircled on all sides by its own steep cliffs rising over 400 metres (1,400 feet) above the Dead Sea it was a natural fortress. During the early part of his reign Herod lived in fear of being deposed by Mark Anthony and later of being overthrown by the Jews. He therefore set about developing the mountain as a last stronghold for himself should the need ever arise.

Around the top he constructed an 18ft high defensive casemate wall two-thirds of a mile long with thirty-eight watchtowers which totally enclosed the summit.

On the cooler northern face he built his own private palace on three terraces with a most luxurious bath and sauna complex nearby. A series of storerooms was constructed adjacent to the palace and filled with enormous reserves of weapons, food, wine and oil. In addition he designed another palace for public ceremonies near the western wall. In order to ensure an adequate water supply a number of large cisterns were carved out of the bedrock capable of holding more than 1,500,000 cu ft of water. By an ingenious system of aqueducts, water from flash floods in the winter was channelled into reservoirs quarried low in the north west of the mountain. From here it was transferred mainly via the water gates to other parts of the fortress.

After Herod's death in 4 BC the mountain remained in Roman hands and was manned by a small garrison. In AD 66 it was captured by Jewish Zealots who set up their own community and converted some of the buildings for religious use including a Synagogue and two Mikve's (ritual immersion pools). The population of Masada grew as freedom fighters joined them from the sacked Holy City.

The Masada Story

According to Flavius Josephus, Jewish historian (c AD 38–100)

Following the fall of Jerusalem in AD 70 the Romans turned their attention to the few remaining pockets of Jewish resistance and the last to be dealt with was Masada. In AD 72 General Flavius Silva himself took command of the

Tenth Legion and set out with 15,000 men including his soldiers, auxiliaries and many prisoners to overthrow the stronghold. He first built eight camps around the base of the mountain together with a siege wall over two miles in length to prevent anyone escaping. The line of these fortifications can still be seen today.

He then began constructing a ramp against the western face of the mountain from which to storm the walls using a mobile siege-tower equipped with catapults, arrow launchers and a giant battering ram. The ramp itself was over 200 metres in length and is still in place today.

In the Spring of AD 73, General Silva's mobile siege tower was drawn up the ramp so that the top of it appeared above the casemate wall forcing the Zealots to take cover. The battering ram was then brought into action and eventually breached the outer wall, but the defenders had hastily constructed an inner wall of timber and earth. The Romans next threw blazing torches down onto this new structure but unexpectedly the wind blew the flames back against their wooden siege tower which was ignited. For a short while the Zealots felt they had been successful in warding off this first attack, but unhappily for them the wind changed again and by nightfall it became clear that their position was hopeless. The 960 men, women and children on Masada were faced with an agonising decision. They had to choose between surrendering to the Romans and submitting themselves to abuse and slavery, or committing mass suicide.

According to Josephus, the Zealot leader Eleazar Ben Yair, called his bravest men together and delivered a powerful and moving oration persuading them that death by their own hands was a more honourable choice than slavery. The speech has been recorded for posterity and the following text is an abridged version of Whiston's translation:

'Since we, long ago, my generous friends, resolved never to be servants to the Romans, nor to any other than to God himself, who alone is the true and just Lord of mankind, the time is now come that obliges us to make that resolution true in practice.

It is very plain that we shall be taken within a day's time; but it is still an eligible thing to die after a glorious manner, together with our dearest friends. This is what our enemies themselves cannot by any means hinder, although they be very desirous to take us alive. Nor can we propose to ourselves any more to fight them and beat them.

Let our wives die before they are abused, and our children before they have tasted of slavery; and after we have slain them, let us bestow that glorious benefit upon one another mutually, and preserve ourselves in freedom, as an excellent funeral monument for us. But first let us destroy our money and the fortress by fire; for I am well assured that this will be a great grief to the Romans, that they shall not be able to seize upon our bodies, and shall fail of our wealth also: and let us spare nothing but our provisions; for they will be a testimonial when we are dead that we were not subdued for want of necessaries; but that we have preferred death before slavery.

We revolted from the Romans with great pretensions to courage; and when at the very last they invited us to preserve ourselves, we would not comply with them. Who will not, therefore, believe that they will certainly be in a rage at us, in case they can take us alive? Miserable will then be the young men, who will be strong enough in their bodies to sustain many torments! Miserable also will be those of elder years, who will not be able to bear those calamities which young men might sustain! One man will be obliged to hear the voice of his son imploring help of his father, when his hands are bound: but certainly our hands are still at liberty, and have a sword in them: let them then be subservient to us in our glorious design; let us die before we become slaves under our enemies, and let us go out of the world, together with our children and our wives, in a state of freedom.' *(Flavius Josephus, 'Jewish War')*

Josephus records that the head of each family, thus persuaded, killed his own wife and children. The remaining men subsequently drew lots to choose ten of their number to slay the rest. After this horrendous task was completed, a further lot was drawn to select one man to put to death the other nine. Finally, having satisfied himself that no one had survived, the last man set fire to their personal possessions and himself committed suicide.

When the Roman soldiers broke into the fortress at daybreak they met no resistance. They must have been amazed to discover the bodies of the 960 men, women and children lying together in their family groups. Theirs was indeed a hollow victory.

Two women and five children evaded the carnage by hiding themselves in a cavern and were thus able to recount the details of that fateful night.

A small garrison from the Tenth Legion remained in occupation for a further forty years before the Romans finally abandoned the mountain. Later, at some time during the fifth/sixth centuries, Masada was occupied by a group of Byzantine monks who built a church on the summit. The remains of this building with its distinctive wall decoration can still be seen today.

There then followed a gap of about 1,400 years when the mountain was forgotten. Over the centuries the precise location of Masada was lost – some scholars were of the opinion that Josephus may even have made up the story – until the site was identified by Edward Robinson and his companion E. Smith in 1838. During the next century various expeditions to Masada were undertaken.

Between October 1963 and April 1965 during the two winter seasons, hundreds of volunteers from twenty-eight countries took part in the world's most ambitious archaeological dig under the direction of Professor Yigael Yadin. The rubble from the collapsed walls and roofs had to be removed before the line of the original Herodian buildings was discovered. Many of the rooms and walls have been partially rebuilt to afford a better idea of the first century layout.

Tour

On arriving at the top cable-car station follow the arrows under the covered way and climb the stone steps, but before mounting the external wooden stairway notice ahead an opening in the mountain face where it is possible to look down into one of the massive man-made water cisterns quarried by Herod's engineers. At some time the water level almost reached the roof. This cistern is one of a number cut into the mountain but is not the largest. Now return to the stairway and mount the sixty-six steps to the admission booth.

Masada is 1,900 feet (570 metres) long and 650 feet (195 metres) wide and there is a great deal to see. If time is limited it is suggested that the numbers on the plan on page 124 are followed as these offer a logical sequence for viewing. Allow a minimum of two hours to visit the more important features whose headings are printed in bold below.

N.B. The black line painted on various walls indicates the level below which archaeologists found the original stone blocks still in place. Above this everything has been painstakingly reconstructed.

(1) Casemate Wall Room
There were originally 110 similar chambers within the defensive walls and towers which were later used to house the Zealots and their families. Notice how the Dead Sea is now divided by a wide stretch of land which has been exposed in recent decades by a dramatic reduction in the water level. This is due to the millions of gallons being drawn off from its only source, the River Jordan, and is causing concern to the environmentalists. From this

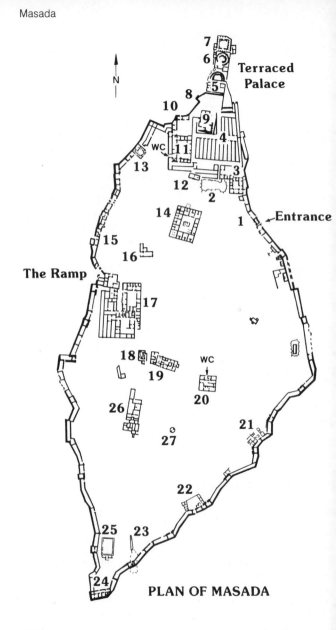

N

Terraced Palace

7
6
8
5
10
9
4
WC
11
3
13
12
2

← **Entrance**

14
1
15
16

The Ramp

17
18
19
WC
20
26
21
27
22
25
23
24

PLAN OF MASADA

vantage point can also be seen in the plain below the position of three of the Roman camps which guarded the eastern approaches to Masada and the line of the siege wall. Within these protective squares the soldiers lived in tents. Various sections of the Snake Path are visible winding to the top.

(2) *Quarry* The stone from here provided Herod's workmen with some of their building material. All the blocks used in his massive construction programme were quarried from the mountain itself.

(3) *Herodian Villa* (Designated Building VIII). One of five erected on the summit, in addition to the two palaces. These were probably intended for the use of Herod's wives or brothers. The three southern rooms here contain some original decoration.

(4) Storerooms There are no fewer than fifteen of these huge rectangular areas within this complex where in addition to a large arsenal of weapons, grain, oil, wine, dates and pulses were kept in their distinctive shaped jars. Originally each room held one particular commodity. Not all the storeroom walls have been reconstructed to their original height of eleven feet. A number have been deliberately left in a ruined state to give visitors an idea of the magnitude of the task which faced the archaeologists.

(5/6/7) Herod's Terraced Palace Villa Built on three separate levels, the top and two lower terraces, in order to take advantage of the cooler northern aspect. The main living accommodation (5) included the area now covered by the viewing platform. The curved line of this modern structure follows precisely the outer bay of the porch of Herod's private palace with its impressive panoramic views. Adjacent to the porch were four ornately decorated dwelling rooms with mosaic floors. This entire palace complex, demanding considerable effort and resources to construct, was designed solely for Herod's personal pleasure and relaxation. It was not intended to accommodate many people.

On the middle terrace (6) stood a circular colonnaded pavilion, while at the lowest level was an elegant rectangular structure (7) also designed for relaxation. This was erected on a man-made platform supported by walls over eighty feet high because the natural rock is only a few yards wide at this point. Preserved here is a fine example of plaster painted to resemble marble. Josephus records that the columns were made in one piece but time has exposed the deception because each is made up of a number of circular stone drums which were then covered in plaster. At this level a small Roman bath-house was also discovered.

It is possible to descend to these terraces via a series of metal stairways the top of which is marked at (8) on the plan. There are 170 steps. Originally internal staircases linked the three levels.

From the viewing platform can be seen the outer walls of the most northern of General Silva's encircling camps.

(8) *Modern Stairway* leading down to the two lower terraces of Herod's northern palace.

(9) Bath-house A most impressive complex in typical Roman style. Note the original painted plaster on the walls of the first room (apoditorium) which was used for disrobing. The next room (tepidarium) was kept warm. Adjacent to this, on the right and at a lower level, was a cold bath (frigidarium). At the end of the wooden walkway is the largest of the chambers which was the hot room (caldarium). This was heated by air circulating under the floor which itself was supported by more than two hundred pedestals. The six feet thick walls were also heated by air from the same source venting through rows of vertical clay pipes which lined the room. The furnace was located immediately outside the wall opposite the viewing platform. High temperatures could be achieved and a considerable

amount of steam produced by splashing the floor and walls with water. Bathers probably wore clogs.

(10) *Water Gate* A path led from here to the reservoirs below.

(11) *Administration Building* used by the Roman garrison. Within its courtyard is a 'Mikve' (ritual immersion bath) constructed later by the Zealots. It comprised a series of three pools for Jewish purification and is one of two found on the mountain.

(12) *Herodian Look-out Tower*

(13) Synagogue Built by Herod for the Jewish members of his entourage and modified by the Zealots, it therefore dates from the Second Temple period and is the oldest yet discovered in Israel. Beneath the floor of the adjacent room were found two parchments inscribed with parts of the books of Deuteronomy and Ezekiel, which are believed to have been buried by the Zealots. Today some young Jewish boys come to Masada to celebrate their Bar Mitzvah.

(14) *Garrison Building* Consisting of an open central courtyard with apartments leading off it. It is thought that during the Herodian period it was occupied by Roman officers and their families. Later it was certainly occupied by the leaders of the Zealot community with their families.

Beneath the floor of one of the dwellings was found a hoard of silver shekels from the period of the Jewish revolt.

(15) Casemate rooms From these rooms along the western wall there is a good view of the Roman assault ramp. Directly across the valley can be seen the seating for the 'Son-et-Lumiere' presentation. Between the two are modern replicas of the siege tower, catapult and battering ram which were used in the epic film on Masada. On the right are two more of the Roman Tenth Legion's camps. The largest was General Silva's Headquarters.

(16) Byzantine Church Dating from the fifth century. A small community of monks, the last known inhabitants of Masada, established themselves here after the earthquake which destroyed many of the buildings. Notice in particular in the nave the original patterned wall decorations of pottery sherds and small stones set in the plaster. In one of the rooms on the north side are some fine floor mosaics.

(17) Western Palace Herod's official residence designed for grand ceremonial occasions, audiences and receptions, this was the largest building on Masada. It comprised three main wings: in the south-east were the royal quarters including the throne room and its entrance hall with a beautiful coloured mosaic floor. Adjacent to this was a small private bath-house with its approach corridor both of which also have fine mosaics. The service wing lay to the north, whilst the western area contained the administrative block and storerooms. The entire complex was designed to be self-sufficient, even to having its own water reservoir. Visitors should not miss the opportunity to climb to the covered viewing platform to look down upon the royal mosaics.

(18) Bathing Pool or Public Bath. The recesses around the upper walls were used to store the bathers' clothes. Steps led right down to the bottom of the pool to enable bathing even when the water was fairly shallow. All the water had to be carried here.

(19) *Herodian Villa* for the use of Herod's family.

(20) *A Royal Residence* Another villa erected specifically for a member of the Royal Family.

(21) *Zealot Quarters* A good example of how the Roman structures were partitioned off by the Zealots to form small simple living units. They made niches in the walls to house their few personal belongings and constructed very basic domestic ovens. Their lifestyle was one of extreme austerity and strict religious observance in contrast to the affluence and luxury of the Romans.

(22) *Casemate Rooms* Immediately adjacent to the 'Bakery' is another room also converted by the Zealots in which can be seen the other 'Mikve', a series of three adjacent pools. One for collecting the rainwater (probably as it drained from the roof) to be used for cleansing; a small bath for washing hands and feet before immersion; and the actual Mikve. Periodic ritual immersion was an essential part of Orthodox Jewish life.

(23) *Water Cistern* The largest of twelve cut into the mountain. This can be viewed by descending 36 steep steps hewn out of the bedrock.

(24) *Southern Citadel* for the defence of this end of the mountain.

(25) *'Great Pool'* There is some doubt about its purpose because it is hardly designed to contain water.

(26) *Southern Villa* A Herodian construction, never completed but converted by the Zealots for their use.

(27) *Columbarium* There are varying opinions about the purpose of this unusual circular structure with its many niches and dividing central wall. Three theories are: (a) pigeon roost; (b) pagan shrine; (c) resting place for cremated human remains. Professor Yadin favoured the latter as the most likely explanation.

Opening Times:
8.00–16.00 daily.
(Fridays 8.00–14.00)
Last cable car down at 17.00
(Fridays 15.00)

Souvenir Shops: Adjacent to the large air-conditioned restaurant near the coach and car park.
Beside the lower cable car station where light refreshment is also available.
There are drinking water taps underneath the cable car station and at numerous positions on the mountain top

Toilets:
(1) Adjoining the large restaurant near the coach and car park;
(2) Beside the lower cable car station;
(3) On the top of the mountain (Marked 'WC' on plan on page 124)

Custodian: The National Parks Authority

Telephone: (07) 584207 (cable car)
(07) 584208 (site office)

Qumran Monastery and Caves

Situated on a sandy plateau at the foot of towering cliffs overlooking the north-western shore of the Dead Sea are the excavated remains of the monastery of the Essenes – a strict religious sect. Here they inscribed their now world-famous 'Dead Sea Scrolls' nearly two thousand years ago. In 1947 some of the hidden manuscripts were accidentally discovered after a young Bedouin goatherd threw a stone into a cave in the escarpment not far from the site. Many scholars are of the opinion that St John the Baptist may have had close connections with the Essenes.

Access

The site is about 45 km due east of Jerusalem. Follow the access instructions for Jericho (see page 114) as far as the Inn of the Good Samaritan. From here descend through the increasingly barren mountains and after 7 km look out on the right for a fairly large milestone inscribed 'Sea Level'. In the tourist season there is sometimes an enterprising Bedouin near it with his camel to attract photographers. Drive on to reach the wide basin of the Jordan Valley; then continue, passing the first turning off to the left leading to Jericho town and the second which is signposted Jericho By-pass, until arriving at the shore of the Dead Sea. Here turn right at the 'T' junction and proceed along the coastal road for a further 7 km until reaching a bus stop where there is a turning off to the right, signposted Qumran. Take this road and the site is straight ahead.

History

There was an Israelite fort here in the eighth century BC but this was abandoned long before a group of Essenes came to the site in the middle of the second century BC. They had broken away from the Temple worship in Jerusalem to embrace a more strict and ascetic way of life. By about 100 BC most of the building had been completed and their numbers had grown to some two hundred. The Monastery itself was used as a centre for worship, study and meals, but it is thought that most of the community lived in caves, shelters or tents nearby.

In 31 BC a major earthquake occurred forcing them to abandon the site for thirty years, but at the beginning of the Christian era members of the sect returned, repaired the damage and remained in occupation until AD 68. During this year, fearing the imminent approach of the conquering Roman soldiers, the community packed their precious parchments into jars and hid them in the nearby

caves. It is thought that some of the Essenes joined up with the Zealots at the top of Masada and no doubt perished there.

Prior to 1950 when archaeologists began to excavate the site following the discovery of the scrolls, the only part of the monastery visible above the sand had been the stub of a watchtower which was locally assumed to be Roman.

The story of how the scrolls were found in the Spring of 1947 is worth briefly recalling: Mohammed Edib, a young Bedouin was searching for one of his lost goats and threw a stone into the opening of a cave thinking that the animal might possibly have strayed inside. The stone made such a strange noise when it hit something that he ran away frightened. The next day he returned with his cousin and the two scrambled down into the cave. They saw eight large earthenware pots and they hoped these might contain gold.

Some of the jars were complete with their sealed lids and it was discovered that they contained in total seven rolls of inscribed parchment. The young Bedouins had no idea of the significance of their find but when they were next visiting Bethlehem they were able to sell them. Three were subsequently purchased by Professor Elazar Sukenik who held the Chair of Archaeology at the Hebrew University in Jerusalem and the other four were sold to Archbishop Samuel of the Syrian Church of St Mark. Two years later the Archbishop took his scrolls to America where he had been advised he would obtain a better price. It transpired that by chance the son of Professor Sukenik, who had adopted the name Yigael Yadin, was visiting the United States and was able to anonymously purchase all four scrolls for $250,000. He immediately returned them to Israel. During further searches of the Dead Sea caves another scroll was found which Yadin was able to acquire in 1967. In all over 900 pieces of manuscript were discovered.

Two of the scrolls are inscribed on copper, the remainder are parchment or papyrus. They include all the books of the Old Testament, except Esther, but the most famous document is the complete text of Isaiah which is one foot wide and 24 feet (8 metres) long. It proved to be one thousand years older than any other known copy. When comparisons were made with two other later documents of the 9/10th centuries they were found to be almost identical, testifying to the accuracy of the scribes throughout the centuries between. A facsimile of this script can be seen in the 'Shrine of the Book' in

Jerusalem which is part of the Israeli National Museum not far from the Knesset Parliament building. Also on view are the 'Thanksgiving Scroll', the scroll of 'The Battle of the Sons of Light against the Sons of Darkness' and the 'Manual of Discipline' setting out in detail the rules of the Qumran Community.

Tour

From the ticket office walk across to the ruins and ascend to the wooden observation platform erected over the original watchtower. All the main features are clearly identified on touring the site, but it is helpful to gain an idea of the layout from this position.

To the south (facing away from the ticket office) and below the tower was a complex of rooms including the Council Chamber indicating that the community was run on democratic lines. Immediately to the left of this is a rectangular room where archaeologists discovered the remains of a plastered table five metres in length and some benches all of which had fallen from the room above known as the 'Scriptorium' where it is thought the scrolls may have been written. They also identified two inkwells, one made of clay and the other of bronze.

Descend the exit steps and follow the arrows round the site. Notice in particular on the left the Assembly Hall and Refectory. Running away from this at right angles is a smaller room which served as a pantry. Here hundreds of bowls stacked in dozens, over 200 plates, a large number of beakers and many other vessels were discovered. Crockery for the everyday use of the community was made on the site.

The Essenes depended for their water upon the rain which drained from the mountains during the winter months. It was channelled via an aqueduct into at least seven storage cisterns within the monastery complex. Some of the reservoirs were probably used as baths for ritual cleansing which was a feature of the religious life of the community.

Archaeologists discovered outside the eastern wall a large burial ground consisting of over 1100 graves in neat lines. Most contain the remains of men, although a few females were also interred.

Continue walking south across the sand to the end of the plateau where on the right will be seen one of the man-made caves in which some 15,000 fragments of parchment were found.

Return to the site to complete the circular tour.

Opening Times:
April to September: 8.00–17.00
October to March: 9.00–16.00
On the eve of Shabbat and holidays closes one hour earlier. Closed on Yom Kippur. The tourist 'Green Card' is accepted

Souvenir Shop: Up the steps from the car park before reaching the ticket office. Large and well stocked. There is an excellent restaurant.

Toilets: Near the ticket office

Custodian: The National Parks Authority

Telephone: (02) 942235

Shrine of the Book in Jerusalem
Opening Times:
Sun. Mon. Weds. Thurs: 10.00–17.00
Tues: 10.00–10.00
Fri & eve of hols: 10.00–14.00
Sat & hols: 10.00–16.00

Telephone: (02) 708811

Jacob's Well

There can be no doubt about the authenticity of this well which was dug by Jacob 3,700 years ago. Here Jesus met the Samaritan woman and spoke to her at length about the 'living water'. Since the fourth century the well has been enclosed within the crypt of a series of churches. The site is situated on the southern approach to the town of Shechem (Nablus), 64 km north of Jerusalem.

Access

From Jerusalem take the main road north for about 60 km and look out for a sign on the left to Shekem and Jenin. Take this road and continue on it for 3 km and then turn sharp right at the green sign for Jiftliq, Jordan Valley and Alon More. In a further 200 metres the entrance gates will be found on the left in a high stone wall.

Details

The earliest church was erected here during the latter part of the fourth century and was mentioned by St Jerome in AD 404. The original building was in the shape of a Latin cross with the ancient well in a crypt under the high altar. This structure was damaged during the Samaritan revolts of the fifth and early sixth centuries, but was completely restored soon afterwards on the orders of the Emperor Justinian. Like other Christian shrines in the Holy Land, it was destroyed by the Persians in 614. In the twelfth century the Crusaders constructed a three-aisled church on part of the Byzantine foundations. After their defeat the building was left to decay.

Meeting with the Samaritan woman (John 4. 4–30)

Jesus had to pass through Samaria, and on his way came to a Samaritan town called Sychar, near the plot of ground which Jacob gave to his son Joseph; Jacob's well was there. It was about noon, and Jesus, tired after his journey, was sitting by the well.

His disciples had gone into the town to buy food. Meanwhile a Samaritan woman came to draw water, and Jesus said to her, 'Give me a drink.' The woman said, 'What! You, a Jew, ask for a drink from a Samaritan woman?' (Jews do not share drinking vessels with Samaritans.) Jesus replied, 'If only you knew what God gives, and who it is that is asking you for a drink, you would have asked him and he would have given you living water.' 'Sir,' the woman said, 'you have no bucket and the well is deep, so where can you get "living water"? Are you greater than Jacob our ancestor who gave us the well and drank from it himself, he and his sons and his cattle too?' Jesus answered, 'Everyone who drinks this water will be thirsty again; but whoever drinks the water I shall give will never again be thirsty. The water that I shall give will be a spring of water within him, welling up and bringing eternal life.' 'Sir,' said the woman, 'give me this water, and then I shall not be thirsty, nor have to come all this way to draw water.'

'Go and call your husband,' said Jesus, 'and come back here.' She answered, 'I have no husband'. Jesus said, 'You are right in saying that you have no husband, for though you have had five husbands, the man you are living with now is not your husband. You have spoken the truth!' 'Sir,' replied the woman, 'I can see you are a prophet. Our fathers worshipped on this mountain, but you Jews say that the place where God must be worshipped is in Jerusalem.' 'Believe me,' said Jesus, 'the time is coming when you will worship the Father neither on this mountain nor in Jerusalem. You Samaritans worship you know not what; we worship what we know. It is from the Jews that salvation comes. But the time is coming, indeed it is already here, when true worshippers will worship the Father in spirit and in truth.' These are the worshippers the Father wants. God is spirit, and those who worship him must worship in spirit and in truth.' The woman answered, 'I know that Messiah' (that is, Christ) 'is coming. When he comes he will make everything clear to us.' Jesus said to her, 'I am he, I who am speaking to you.'

At that moment his disciples returned, and were astonished to find him talking with a woman; but none of them said, 'What do you want?' or, 'Why are you talking with her?' The woman left her water-jar and went off to the town, where she said to the people, 'Come and see a man who has told me everything I ever did. Could this be the Messiah?' They left the town and made their way towards him. (REB)

'He feeds the hungry with the Bread of heaven,
And living streams to those who thirst are given.'

In the sixteenth century it is recorded that the Franciscans celebrated an annual Mass within the ruins, and a century later the Greek Orthodox from Sebaste occasionally conducted their liturgy at the site. Finally in 1860 the Greeks acquired the property and immediately set about restoring the crypt. It was not until 1914 however that work commenced on the construction of a substantial church above it with funds provided by the Pravoslav Church of Czarist Russia, but the Revolution of 1917 brought the project to an abrupt halt.

It is this impressive but incomplete building which the pilgrim sees today. The massive nave pillars and unfinished walls stand unroofed and remain open to the skies. Entrance to the crypt containing Jacob's Well is via one of two staircases temporarily protected by wooden structures resembling sentry boxes. The well has an exceptional depth of 35 metres and is the only one in the area. The Greek Orthodox priest on duty will be happy to let down the bucket by means of a simple metal winch to draw up the cool clear drinking water.

From the site, looking to the left, there is an excellent view of Mount Gerizim which is the Holiest Place for the ancient Samaritan sect who still worship on its summit, rather than in Jerusalem. To the right is Mount Ebal.

Opening Times:
9.00–12.00 daily
Ring the bell

Souvenir Shop: In the crypt

Toilets: Near the entrance gate

Custodian: The Greek Orthodox Church

Telephone: (05) 375123

Sea of Galilee

The tranquillity of this beautiful Lake cannot fail to delight the pilgrim and provide a store of lifetime memories. It is still a very special place for the Christian in spite of modern developments and the outline of the surrounding hills has changed little since Our Lord walked upon these Galilean shores.

The Lake which lies 200 metres (660 feet) below the level of the Mediterranean Sea is approximately 21 km (15 miles) long by 12 km (8 miles) wide. Its maximum depth is 50 metres (165 feet).

Some initial confusion is caused by the fact that it is referred to by so many different names. To Christians it is generally known as the 'Sea of Galilee', but road signs direct travellers to 'Lake Kinnereth' (derived from the Hebrew word for a harp). St Matthew, St Mark and St John all mention the 'Sea of Galilee', although St John also calls it the 'Sea of Tiberias'. St Luke refers to 'Lake Gennesaret', whilst in J. G. Whittier's popular hymn 'Dear Lord and Father of Mankind' it becomes the 'Syrian Sea'.

Most of Our Lord's lakeside ministry – as recorded in the four Gospels – was confined to the northern half. In his day the area was densely populated with possibly as many as seven large towns and a thriving fishing industry.

It was also on one of the major trade routes between the east and the west. The pilgrim today is reminded of so many incidents in the Gospel story:

– Fishermen can still be seen standing in the shallow waters near the shore casting their nets in the traditional fashion, while others set off in boats at sunset to fish at night.

– Violent storms sometimes develop in the mid-afternoon as the cooler air rushes down from the surrounding mountains and whips up the water to produce enormous waves. Then, in a relatively short time there is a great calm again.

– The wheat and the tares still grow together in fields around the lake, and in Springtime there is a profusion of wild flowers to remind the pilgrim of Our Lord's words: 'even Solomon in all his glory was not arrayed like one of these'.

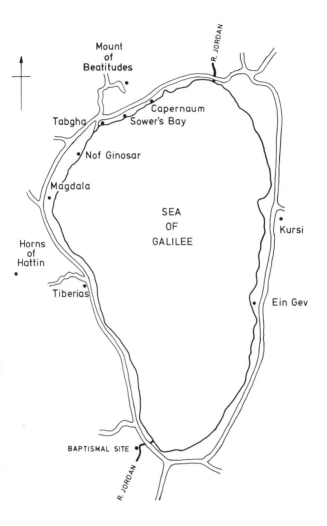

Sketch map of the Sea of Galilee referred to on most road signs and maps as 'Lake Kinneret'.

- The twinkling lights from the medieval City of Safed, high up in the northern mountains, are an illustration of his comment: 'A city that is set on a hill cannot be hid'.

- The dawn chorus in the trees surrounding the lake, and the truly unforgettable pink hue across the water just before the sun rises, are all wonders that Jesus himself experienced in this very place.

Around the shores are many places of interest to the Christian pilgrim. Looking at the map and reading clockwise from Tiberias, these are:

The Horns of Hattin The name given to a long low hill with a hump on either end resembling horns (when seen from the main road travelling west from Tiberias). Here the Crusaders were inexorably defeated by Saladin in a horrendous battle on 4th July 1187.

Magdala According to tradition the birthplace of Mary Magdalene. About 5 km north of Tiberias between the main road and the sea are some excavations. The fenced compound is owned by the Franciscans but is not open to the public. In Our Lord's time there was an important fishing port here. Indeed, both the Hebrew and Greek names for the town made reference to the fish. Towards the end of the first century the historian Flavius Josephus mentions a population of 40,000 with a fleet of 230 boats.

Nof Ginosar Within the grounds of a modern hotel and Kibbutz are preserved the remains of a first century fishing boat which was discovered in 1986 when the

---

Stilling the Storm (Matt 8. 23–27)

And when he was entered into a ship, his disciples followed him. And behold, there arose a great tempest in the sea, insomuch that the ship was covered with the waves: but he was asleep. And his disciples came to him, and awoke him, saying, 'Lord, save us: we perish'. And he saith unto them, 'Why are ye fearful, O ye of little faith?' Then he arose, and rebuked the winds and the sea; and there was a great calm. But the men marvelled, saying, 'What manner of man is this, that even the winds and the sea obey him!' (AV)

'When fears appal and faith is failing,
Make thy voice heard o'er wind and wave;
And in thy perfect love prevailing
Put forth thy hand to help and save.'

For further Gospel references, see page 196

water of the lake was particularly low. This prosperous establishment is possibly on the site of another important fishing port, Gennesaret, from which the Lake took one of its names in New Testament times.

Tabgha The traditional site of the 'Feeding of the Five Thousand' and of Jesus's Resurrection appearance to the Disciples when he cooked breakfast for them on the seashore after they had been fishing all night. (*See details on page 145.*)

The Mount of Beatitudes Almost directly behind Tabgha on higher ground is the place where the 'Sermon on the Mount' is commemorated. (*See details on page 143.*)

Chorazin 3½ km due north of the Mount of Beatitudes. One of the three towns condemned by Jesus for failing to repent. Archaeological excavations have revealed the remains of a synagogue. The site is open to the public.

Sower's Bay 1 km east of Tabgha. A possible site of Our Lord's 'Parable of the Sower' and other teachings. (*See details on page 150.*)

Capernaum Our Lord's adopted 'home town' and having more Gospel references than any other place in the Holy Land. (*See details on page 151.*)

The River Jordan 4km to the east of Capernaum the river can be seen passing under a road bridge. From here it flows on to enter the Sea of Galilee about 1 km further south. The Jordan continues its course from the southern end of the lake where there is a modern Baptismal site. (*See details on page 141.*)

Bethsaida The other town, in addition to Chorazin and Capernaum, condemned by Jesus for failing to repent. It seems likely that this was situated to the east of the point where the River Jordan joins the lake. The site is covered by water and a swamp, consequently excavations have still to be carried out. (Healing of the blind man: Mark 8.22–26.)

Kursi On the eastern side of the lake, almost opposite Magdala, and inland of the main road are the impressive remains of a fine Byzantine church and monastery dating from the fifth century. The site is open to the public. Traditionally this area is associated with the story of the Gadarene swine. Jesus having cleansed a tormented man of evil spirits, transferred them to a large herd of swine grazing nearby. Being thus possessed they ran headlong down the hillside into the sea and were drowned. (Matthew 8.28–33; Mark 5.1–20; Luke 8.26–39)

Hippos 5 km further south of Kursi, on the summit of a hill directly behind the Kibbutz at Ein Gev, is the site of this ancient fortified town dating from 332 BC. Although now overgrown, the outline of its foundations can just be identified from the road. The site is of particular interest to the Christian pilgrim because it seems quite probable that this is the place which Our Lord had in mind when he said: 'A city that is set on a hill cannot be hid'.

Opening Times of Chorazin and Kursi:
Summer: 8.00–17.00 (Fridays closes at 16.00)
Winter: 8.00–16.00 (Fridays 9.00–15.00). Closed on Yom Kippur.
The tourist 'green card' is accepted

Souvenir Shops: None

Toilets: In the car parks

Custodian: The National Parks Authority

Telephone: Chorazin (06) 934982
Kursi   (06) 731983

River Jordan

There are five different locations where, according to various traditions, Jesus was baptised. At the time of writing, most of them are in forbidden military zones, but a modern site commemorating the event has been built on the riverside at the southern end of the Sea of Galilee.

Access from Tiberias (see map on page 137)

Travel south on the lakeside road and after 8 km look out for a signpost on the right to the Baptismal Place. The turning is just before the bridge over the River Jordan (Gesher Yarden) and the site is about 200 metres from the main road.

Details

An extensive baptismal place has been constructed on the river bank adjoining purpose-built facilities which comprise a large car park, snack bar, souvenir shop, changing rooms and toilets.

If the place is too crowded, it is possible as an alternative to scramble down to the river from the roadway beyond the Jordan Bridge, but devotions can be interrupted by traffic noise.

A quieter location is at the northern end of the lake 19km from Tiberias. Follow the access instructions for Capernaum on page 151 as far as the Lido, but instead of turning right at this point keep straight on for another 4 km. Turn right at the signpost to the 'Arique Bridge'. Here the banks are in a natural setting but there is a steep and rather difficult approach to the water.

Authors' Comments

The site in the south is conveniently near Tiberias, but it is run as a commercial enterprise. Nevertheless, on a quiet day, it can be a pleasant place set amidst the prolific vegetation of the river bank. The northern alternative, although much further away, is totally unspoilt.

Opening Times:
Southern site: 8.00–17.00

Souvenir Shop:
Large and well stocked

Toilets: Changing rooms also available

Custodian: The State Tourism Corporation

Telephone: (06) 759486

The Baptism of Jesus (Mark 1. 4–11)

John did baptize in the wilderness, and preach the baptism of repentance for the remission of sins. And there went out unto him all the land of Judaea, and they of Jerusalem, and were all baptized of him in the River of Jordan, confessing their sins. And John was clothed with camel's hair, and with a girdle of a skin about his loins; and he did eat locusts and wild honey; and preached, saying, 'There cometh one mightier than I after me, the latchet of whose shoes I am not worthy to stoop down and unloose. I indeed have baptized you with water: but he shall baptize you with the Holy Ghost'. And it came to pass in those days, that Jesus came from Nazareth of Galilee, and was baptized of John in Jordan. And straightway coming up out of the water, he saw the heavens opened, and the spirit, like a dove, descending upon him. And there came a voice from heaven, saying, 'Thou art my beloved Son, in whom I am well pleased'. (AV)

'So when the Dove descended
on him, The Son of Man,
the hidden years had ended,
the age of grace began.'

For further Gospel references, see page 197

Mount of Beatitudes

In a delightful setting overlooking the Sea of Galilee from its northern shore, Our Lord's Sermon on the Mount is commemorated. The colonnaded terrace of the distinctive twentieth century Italian church, built on the brow of a hill, affords magnificent panoramic views across the lake.

Access from Tiberias (see map on page 137)

The site is about 16 km from the town. Drive north on the lake ring road. After 11 km ascend the hill passing by an electricity grid station. Keep straight on at the Kefar Nahum junction and in a further 2 km climb another hill negotiating three sharp bends. Shortly afterwards look out for a sign on the right to The Hospice of Beatitudes. The site is reached in about 1 km. Parking space is available in front of the main gates.

Details

The land was acquired in 1926 by The National Association for Aid to Italian Missionaries. They built a hospice here to enable pilgrims to spend time in contemplation and prayer.

The church was constructed in 1937 to a design by the Italian architect Antonio Barluzzi who was responsible for so many expressive buildings in the Holy Land. The style is typically Italian and the interior is symbolically octagonal. The centrally placed altar is surmounted by a slender arch of alabaster and onyx. There are fine views of the surrounding countryside through the narrow horizontal windows in the lower walls, while in the upper windows are written the eight Beatitudes from Our Lord's Sermon. The mosaics in the

143

floor represent the seven virtues which he mentioned. In the landscaped garden outside there are three altars for group worship.

Authors' Comments

This is undoubtedly one of the most beautiful Gospel sites in the Holy Land and a visit here should not be rushed.

Opening Times: 8.00–12.00 14.30–17.00 daily

Souvenir Shop: Just inside the Church on the right

Toilets: In the garden to the right of the hostel

Custodian: The Franciscan Missionary Sisters of the Immaculate Heart of Mary

Telephone: (06) 790978

The Beatitudes (Matthew 5. 1–12)

Seeing the multitudes, Jesus went up into a mountain: and when he was set, his disciples came unto him: and he opened his mouth, and taught them, saying:

Blessed are the poor in spirit: for their's is the kingdom of heaven.
Blessed are they that mourn: for they shall be comforted.
Blessed are the meek: for they shall inherit the earth.
Blessed are they which do hunger and thirst after righteousness: for they shall be filled.
Blessed are the merciful: for they shall obtain mercy.
Blessed are the pure in heart: for they shall see God.
Blessed are the peacemakers: for they shall be called the children of God.
Blessed are they which are persecuted for righteousness' sake: for their's is the kingdom of heaven.
Blessed are ye, when men shall revile you, and persecute you, and shall say all manner of evil against you falsely, for my sake. Rejoice, and be exceeding glad: for great is your reward in heaven: for so persecuted they the prophets which were before you. (AV)

'Lord, we thy presence seek;
may ours this blessing be;
give us a pure and lowly heart,
a temple meet for thee.'

For further Gospel references, see page 195

Tabgha

Church of the Multiplication
Church of Mensa Christi

The word Tabgha is a corruption of the Greek words *Hepta pegon* (seven springs) and these still exist in the area. There are two major sites in this small fertile oasis on the north-western shore of the Sea of Galilee.

1. The modern Church of the Multiplication commemorates the place where, according to tradition, Jesus fed the 5000 with five loaves and two small fishes. Incorporated into its floor are some particularly fine fifth century mosaics which are considered to be among the loveliest in the Holy Land.

2. Nearby is the little chapel of 'Mensa Christi' (Table of Christ), also known as 'Peter's Primacy', built upon a rock at the water's edge. Traditionally, this is where Jesus appeared to the disciples on the lakeside after his Resurrection.

Access from Tiberias *(see map on page 137)*

Tabgha is about 13 km from Tiberias and is situated at the top of the Sea of Galilee. Drive north on the lake ring road. After 11 km ascend the hill passing by an electricity grid station. Turn right at the Kefar Nahum junction and in about 100 metres, at a smaller junction, keep to the left. Ahead on the right amongst some trees is the Church of the Multiplication where ample parking space is available.

The chapel of 'Mensa Christi' is a further 200 metres along the road on the right. There is a small parking area opposite. The two buildings are not directly linked by any footpath.

*   *   *

THE CHURCH OF THE MULTIPLICATION

FEEDING OF THE FIVE THOUSAND

History

The first church on the site was very small and built circa AD 350. One hundred and thirty years later it was superseded by a much larger basilica which had a central nave and two side aisles. After the Persian invasion in 614 and the subsequent occupation of Palestine by the Arabs, this church fell into ruins. There is no record of any Crusader building here in the twelfth century and it was not until 1932 that the area was excavated. Shortly

afterwards the Benedictines erected a fairly plain church and this in turn was demolished to make way for the present building which was completed in 1984.

Tour

Walk across the pleasant courtyard into the cloister where, on the wall which faces the church, is displayed an archaeological diagram

---

Feeding of the Five Thousand (John 6. 1–13)

Jesus withdrew to the farther shore of the sea of Galilee and a large crowd of people followed him because they had seen the signs he performed in healing the sick. Jesus went up the hillside and sat down with his disciples. It was near the time of Passover, the great Jewish festival.

Looking up and seeing a large crowd coming towards him, Jesus said to Philip, 'Where are we to buy bread to feed these people?' He said this to test him; Jesus himself knew what he meant to do. Philip replied, 'We would need two hundred denarii to buy enough bread for each of them to have a little.' One of his disciples, Andrew, the brother of Simon Peter, said to him, 'There is a boy here who has five barley loaves and two fish; but what is that among so many?' Jesus said, 'Make the people sit down.' There was plenty of grass there, so the men sat down, about five thousand of them. Then Jesus took the loaves, gave thanks, and distributed them to the people as they sat there. He did the same with the fish, and they had as much as they wanted. When everyone had had enough, he said to his disciples, 'Gather up the pieces left over, so that nothing is wasted.' They gathered them up, and filled twelve baskets with the pieces of the five barley loaves that were left uneaten. (REB)

'Thou who dost give us earthly bread,
Give us the Bread eternal.'

For further Gospel references, see page 198

showing the positions of the three previous buildings and the history of the site. Notice that the small original church was set at a different angle from the other two. The fine bronze west doors depict various events in the ministry of Jesus, and to the right of this is a casting, also in bronze, delineating the positions of the three earlier churches.

The principal feature of the present building is the famous fifth century mosaic in front of the main altar depicting a basket of loaves flanked by two fishes. The ancient stone under the altar is reputed to be part of the one upon which Jesus placed the loaves and fishes.

On either side of the altar in the floor of the two side aisles and to the left of the nave are extensive areas of beautiful mosaics depicting numerous birds amongst the flora and water-vegetation. It is possible to identify herons, cranes, ducks, geese, cormorants, peacocks, a flamingo and a swan. There are also a number of geometric designs, copies of those which covered the remaining floor area of the fifth century building.

On the south side of the church is a Benedictine Monastery built in 1956. Here they specialise in caring for disabled young people by providing them with an opportunity for a holiday beside the lake during the summer months.

Authors' Comments

The modern church and cloister are a very pleasant setting in which to reflect upon one of Our Lord's best known miracles.

Opening Times:
8.30–17.00 daily
(Sundays: opens at 10.00)

Souvenir Shop: In the cloister

Toilets: In the car park

Custodian: A German Benedictine Catholic Community

Telephone: (06) 721061

* * *

CHURCH OF 'MENSA CHRISTI' or 'PETER'S PRIMACY'

THE TABLE OF CHRIST OR THE COMMISSIONING OF PETER

A small Franciscan chapel built over an area of rock at the water's edge commemorating the Resurrection appearance of Jesus to his Disciples. They had been fishing all night and had caught nothing. There is an ancient tradition that this was the rock upon which Our Lord prepared breakfast for them. After the meal Jesus commissioned Peter with the words: 'Feed my sheep'.

Access

From the entrance to the Church of the Multiplication

147

continue along the main road
for about 200 metres. The
gates are on the right.

History

Although the Franciscans
have discovered the remains
of an early building on the
rock, there is no documentary
evidence of a church here
until the ninth century.

Breakfast on the Seashore (John 21. 1–14)

*Some time later, Jesus showed himself to his disciples once again, by the
sea of Tiberias. This is how it happened. Simon Peter was with Thomas
the twin, Nathanael from Cana-in-Galilee, the sons of Zebedee, and two
other disciples. 'I am going out fishing,' said Simon Peter. 'We will go
with you,' said the others. So they set off and got into the boat; but that
night they caught nothing.*

*Morning came, and Jesus was standing on the beach, but the disciples did
not know that it was Jesus. He called out to them, 'Friends, have you
caught anything?' 'No,' they answered. He said, 'Throw out the net to
starboard, and you will make a catch.' They did so, and found they could
not haul the net on board, there were so many fish in it. Then the disciple
whom Jesus loved said to Peter, 'It is the Lord!' As soon as Simon Peter
heard him say, 'It is the Lord,' he fastened his coat about him (for he had
stripped) and plunged into the sea. The rest of them came on in the boat,
towing the net full of fish. They were only about a hundred yards from
land.*

*When they came ashore, they saw a charcoal fire there with fish laid on it,
and some bread. Jesus said, 'Bring some of the fish you have caught.'
Simon Peter went on board and hauled the net to land; it was full of big
fish, a hundred and fifty-three in all; and yet, many as they were, the net
was not torn. Jesus said, 'Come and have breakfast.' None of the disciples
dared to ask 'Who are you?' They knew it was the Lord. Jesus came, took
the bread and gave it to them, and the fish in the same way. This makes
the third time that Jesus appeared to his disciples after his resurrection
from the dead.* (REB)

> 'In simple trust like theirs who heard,
> beside the Syrian sea,
> the gracious calling of the Lord,
> let us, like them, without a word
> rise up and follow thee.'

For further Gospel references, see page 198

Nevertheless, in AD 383 the Nun Egeria mentions some steps upon which the Lord stood. There are some ancient steps cut into the south face of the rock close to the water's edge.

In the twelfth century there was certainly a church here but, like other Christian buildings on the shores of Galilee, it appears to have fallen into ruins after the defeat of the Crusaders. In 1933 the Franciscans built the present chapel using the dark basalt rock which is so plentiful in the area.

Details

On the right just inside the entrance to the site can be seen the ruins of a Byzantine water tower, one of a number in the area. Continue along the path through the garden to the little chapel. Opposite the west door is an area designed for group worship and between this and the lake is a modern bronze statue of Jesus symbolically commissioning Peter with his shepherd's crook.

Inside the simple chapel, the striking feature is the extensive granite rock running across its entire width. According to tradition it was here that Jesus made his Resurrection appearance to the Disciples on the lakeside.

Authors' Comments

A truly delightful site at the water's edge which lends itself to meditation and prayer.

Opening Times:
8.00–18.00 daily
(Winter: closes 17.00)
Souvenir Shop: None
Toilets: To the left of the garden
Custodian: The Franciscans
Telephone: (06) 724767

Sower's Bay

1km due east of Mensa Christi is a bay which possesses all the characteristics of a natural amphitheatre. On a fine day – when there is no wind and little traffic – it is possible to stand at the water's edge and read the Parable of the Sower which can be heard quite clearly from the roadside. This parable and a number of others were preached from a boat and from such a place therefore Jesus would have addressed the multitude.

Parable of the Sower (Mark 4. 1–9)

On another occasion Jesus began to teach by the lakeside. The crowd that gathered round him was so large that he had to get into a boat on the lake and sit there, with the whole crowd on the beach right down to the water's edge. And he taught them many things by parables. As he taught he said:

'Listen! A sower went out to sow. And it happened that as he sowed, some of the seed fell along the footpath; and the birds came and ate it up. Some fell on rocky ground, where it had little soil, and it sprouted quickly because it had no depth of earth; but when the sun rose it was scorched, and as it had no root it withered away. Some fell among thistles; and the thistles grew up and choked the corn, and it produced no crop. And some of the seed fell into good soil, where it came up and grew, and produced a crop; and the yield was thirtyfold, sixtyfold, even a hundredfold.' He added, 'If you have ears to hear, then hear.' (REB)

'Speak to us, O Lord, believing,
as we hear, the sower sows;
may our hearts, your word receiving,
be the good ground where it grows.'

For further Gospel references, see pages 197–8

Capernaum

This partially excavated archaeological site is of major importance to Christians because Capernaum was adopted by Jesus as his 'home town' after he was driven out of Nazareth. Here he called Peter, Andrew, James, John, and Matthew to follow him, and performed a number of miracles. He worshipped and taught in the synagogue. From this busy fishing port and frontier post on the main route to Damascus he chose to carry out the major part of his ministry.

Today its two main features are the partly reconstructed late fourth century synagogue, built upon the foundations of the one in which Our Lord preached, and the contrasting late twentieth century church erected over the site of a house claimed by the Franciscans to have been the home of St Peter.

Access from Tiberias (see map on page 137)

Capernaum is about 15 km from Tiberias and is situated at the top of the Sea of Galilee in the middle of its northern shore. Drive north on the lake ring road. After 11 km ascend the hill passing by an electricity grid station. Turn right at the Kefar Nahum junction and in about 100 metres at a smaller junction keep to the left. Ahead on the right are the two churches at Tabgha, and 1 km beyond them is 'Sower's Bay'. If not stopping at the Bay, continue along the lakeside road for another 1 km and then look out for a turning off to the right, by a Lido, which leads directly to Capernaum where ample parking facilities are available. The car park is beyond the coach park.

General

Capernaum fell into disuse over a thousand years ago. During the nineteenth century scholars began to take some interest in the scattered ruins and in 1894 the Franciscans purchased part of the site. A number of different excavations took place at the beginning of the twentieth century centered on the synagogue and the remains of a fifth century octagonal church, but it was not until 1968 that more intensive work commenced. Archaeologists then discovered the 'Peter House' under the octagonal church, and the remains of shops and other dwellings undoubtedly familiar to Our Lord. To date only a comparatively small part of the town which had a lakeside frontage of about half a kilometre has been excavated.

The area is relatively small and, rather like the Church of the Holy Sepulchre or the Crusader Upper Room in Jerusalem, Capernaum is on the main tourist route. At peak times it is not unusual to see a dozen or more coaches parked and the site can become somewhat overcrowded. In the high season try to arrive early or at lunchtime.

To the east of the walled compound there is a small Greek Orthodox Church,

identified by its red domes. However this can only be approached by a rough track from the main road.

Tour

Inside the first entrance gate and on the left is a small garden in which there is a bronze statue of St Francis. To the right of the pathway is a building which at one time was inhabited by the Franciscans. Inside the second archway and on the right is an office where entrance tickets are sold and a limited number of souvenirs. From here walk diagonally across to the remains of the Old Synagogue.

In 1923 an effort was made to reconstruct the building from the profusion of material on the site. It is thought that this synagogue was probably the most ornate in the whole of Galilee. The white limestone came from a local quarry. Some fine carved pieces are displayed featuring flowers, grapes, pomegranates, and particularly the date palm which is a symbol of the land. There are also a number of geometric designs including the 'Star of David'.

Before ascending the steps into the main prayer hall notice on the left the black basalt volcanic rock foundations upon which this late fourth century 'White Synagogue' was built. It is now almost certain that these earlier remains are part of the building which Jesus knew so well.

Ascend the steps and enter the rectangular prayer hall. It is thought that there may have been a gallery supported by a row of columns running down either side and across the far end. Adjoining the right hand side of the main hall are the remains of an open courtyard which was added a century later. Pass through the archway into this area. The courtyard was enclosed on three sides by a colonnaded cloister. Walk across to the far side from where can be seen the outline of a first century street with a number of shops.

Before finally leaving the synagogue walk through one of the reconstructed portals and notice immediately below, the excavated walls of houses built of the dark basalt volcanic rocks which are so plentiful in the region. These simple dwellings date from the beginning of the first century and would also have been familiar to Jesus.

It is interesting to note that many of the houses follow a standard pattern in which a number of low roofed rooms with windows facing inwards, surrounded an open courtyard. Some of the door and window lintels have now been reconstructed, albeit nearer the ground, to give an idea of the layout. The fairly primitive roofs would have been made of wooden beams covered with a mixture of beaten earth and straw. One is reminded of the story of the sick man being let down through the roof to be healed by Jesus. Access was via a flight of stone steps and some of the lower ones are still visible.

The courtyard itself played a very important part in the life of the family. Here they cooked, ate their meals, and worked at their crafts. During the hot summer months when there was no rain, they probably slept on mats laid out on the compressed soil. The small rooms were used for storage, although in the rainy season or in case of sickness, these provided shelter.

Between the synagogue and the sea stands the modern Roman Catholic Church completed in June 1990 and dedicated to St Peter. It was designed by the Italian Architect Ildo Avetta of Rome whose objective was twofold: first, to provide a place of worship within this important Gospel site; and secondly, to protect the excavated remains of a fifth century church and 'Peter House'.

The Franciscan archaeologists, mainly Fr's Virgilio Corbo and Stanislao Loffreda, who have carried out a very thorough study of the site, believe that this Byzantine Church was built over the family home of Peter and that here Jesus often stayed. The archaeologists claim that the house dates from before the Birth of Christ. In the late first century AD the courtyard was apparently used as a 'Domus-Ecclesia' (house church) by the early Judeo-Christians. This is borne out by the fact that, unlike other buildings so far uncovered in the town, the floor was relaid in lime several times during the first to fourth centuries, and the walls were replastered on a number of occasions. They discovered over one hundred inscriptions in Greek, Aramaic and Hebrew, and the words 'Jesus', 'Lord' and 'Christ' appeared several times. The name 'Peter' occurred at least twice and at the lowest level some fish-hooks were unearthed.

In the fourth century this 'Domus Ecclesia' was enlarged and enclosed within a wall. Finally, in the latter half of the fifth century an octagonal church was built over the whole area with the centre exactly above the foundations of the original courtyard. The outline of this ancient octagon has been faithfully followed by the new church.

The present ultra-modern structure rests upon eight sturdy pillars to avoid damage to the excavated Byzantine foundations below. Reinforced concrete has been used to withstand earthquakes and, in an attempt to blend it with its surroundings, this has been

faced with local basalt. For the same reason the roof has been covered in lead.

At the time of writing visitors are not permitted to enter the Church, apart from Roman Catholic groups who may celebrate Mass here by prior arrangement with the Franciscan authorities. Nevertheless it is possible to view the foundations of the octagonal church and the 'Peter House' without entering the building.

Before leaving Capernaum take the opportunity to examine the exhibits laid out in the area between the synagogue and the ticket office. Of particular interest are an oil press and grinding stones made of black basalt rock. There are also some fine carvings in white limestone along the southern boundary. To the left of the central feature in this display is an interesting carving of the Ark of the Covenant looking rather like a traditional gipsy caravan. It is a unique representation showing how the Tablets of

the Law were transported by the tribes of Israel before they finally came to rest in the Temple in Jerusalem.

Opening Times:
8.30–16.15 daily

Souvenir Shop: Mainly postcards in the ticket office

Toilets: In the car park

Custodian: The Franciscans. There is a charge for admission

Telephone: (06) 721059

Authors' Comments

The fourth century Synagogue is impressive and the excavated remains on the site are also interesting because here one is seeing many objects that were familiar to Jesus. When the area is free of tourists it is possible to capture a little of the atmosphere of this very special place.

The Healing of the Paralytic (Mark 2. 1–12)

After some days Jesus returned to Capernaum, and news went round that he was at home; and such a crowd collected that there was no room for them even in the space outside the door. While he was proclaiming the message to them, a man was brought who was paralysed. Four men were carrying him, but because of the crowd they could not get him near. So they made an opening in the roof over the place where Jesus was, and when they had broken through they lowered the bed on which the paralysed man was lying. When he saw their faith, Jesus said to the man, 'My son, your sins are forgiven.'

Now there were some scribes sitting there, thinking to themselves, 'How can the fellow talk like that? It is blasphemy! Who but God can forgive sins?' Jesus knew at once what they were thinking, and said to them, 'Why do you harbour such thoughts? Is it easier to say to this paralysed man, "Your sins are forgiven," or to say, "Stand up, take your bed, and walk"? But to convince you that the Son of Man has authority on earth to forgive sins' – he turned to the paralysed man – 'I say to you, stand up, take your bed, and go home.' And he got up, and at once took his bed and went out in full view of them all, so that they were astounded and praised God. 'Never before', they said, 'have we seen anything like this.' (REB)

'Manifest in making whole
Palsied limbs and fainting soul;
Anthems be to thee addressed,
God in Man made manifest.'

For further Gospel references, see pages 195–6

Caesarea Philippi

(Modern name: Banias)

The area is at the extreme northern tip of Israel and is of Christian significance because both the Gospels of St Matthew and St Mark record that Jesus came here with his Disciples. The site is now within a National Nature Park and includes one of the three main sources of the River Jordan which flows out below a rugged cliff. There is a tradition that it was here that Jesus referred to St Peter as the 'rock'.

Access from Tiberias

About 60 km due north of the town. Make for Qiryat Shemona (46 km) passing the town on the left and soon afterwards take the road to the right. The site is another 12 km on the left.

History

The area is now called Banias which is an Arab corruption of the earlier name 'Panias'. There was a city here in the first century BC dedicated to the pagan god Pan who in ancient Greece was reputed to protect flocks and herds. The Roman Emperor Augustus gave the city to Herod the Great who built an elaborate palace in his honour. After Herod's death his youngest son Philip, who became Tetrarch of Galilee, renamed the city Caesarea Philippi to distinguish it from Caesarea on the coast and made his headquaters here. Later there was a Christian community in the city which suffered much persecution in a predominantly pagan environment. Nevertheless it is recorded that their bishops attended Councils of the Church in the fourth and fifth centuries. Even after the Persian conquest in the seventh century, it remained a prosperous place on account of its position on the road to Damascus. Later the Crusaders improved the fortifications. Very little has so far been excavated although there is much carved stone lying around.

Three kilometres to the west are the remains of the city of Dan which is archaeologically more interesting. 'Dan to Beersheba' was how the length of the land was described in the Old Testament.

Details

The region is in the southern foothills of Mount Hermon whose tall peak rises 2814 metres (9232 feet) above sea level. The site of Banias is owned by the Israeli authorities and is well preserved as a nature park. There is a fairly expensive entrance fee and the 'green card' used by tourists to gain admission to archaeological sites is not accepted. Within the pleasant compound is a restaurant, and also a gift shop specialising in posters and postcards of the local flora and fauna. There are a

---

Peter's Commissioning (Matt 16. 13–20)

When Jesus came into the coasts of Caesarea Philippi, he asked his disciples, saying, 'Whom do men say that I, the Son of man, am?' And they said, 'Some say that thou art John the Baptist; some, Elias; and others, Jeremias, or one of the prophets'. He saith unto them, 'But whom say ye that I am?' And Simon Peter answered and said, 'Thou art the Christ, the Son of the living God'. And Jesus answered and said unto him, 'Blessed art thou, Simon Bar-jona: for flesh and blood hath not revealed it unto thee, but my Father which is in heaven. And I say also unto thee, that thou art Peter; and upon this rock I will build my church; and the gates of hell shall not prevail against it. And I will give unto thee the keys of the kingdom of heaven: and whatsoever thou shalt bind on earth, shall be bound in heaven; and whatsoever thou shalt loose on earth, shall be loosed in heaven'. Then charged he his disciples, that they should tell no man that he was Jesus the Christ. (AV)

'O Rock of ages, one Foundation
On which the living Church doth rest
Thy name be blest.'

For further Gospel references, see page 195

number of signposted walks beside the fast flowing waters which at this point are known as the River Hermon.

The main feature is a massive rockface below which the extremely cold water emerges having started its journey as the melting snows of Mount Hermon. Take the steep path leading up to the base of the escarpment and notice that cut into it are some ornamental niches which originally contained statues of the pagan god Pan. It seems most likely that Jesus and his disciples would have been familiar with these shrines. The water originally flowed out of the cave to the left, but an earthquake has caused a landslide to block the entrance and it now emerges at a lower level.

There is a tradition that this rock is the one which prompted Jesus to say to St Peter: 'You are Peter, and on this rock I will build my Church'.

Authors' Comments

There are no Christian churches in the region, but if the weather is fine a visit is well worthwhile to enjoy the unspoilt countryside and see one of the three main sources of the River Jordan.

Opening Times: 8.00–17.00 Winter closes at 16.00 On the eve of Shabbat and holidays closes one hour earlier. Closed on Yom Kippur

Souvenir Shop: Near the car park. About 100 metres on the left is a snack bar and restaurant

Toilets: Opposite the restaurant

Custodian: The Nature Reserve Authority of Israel

Telephone: (06) 950272

Mount Tabor

Since the fourth century this dome-shaped mountain rising 450 metres (1,500 feet) above the Plain of Jezreel has been venerated as the traditional site of the Transfiguration.

Access

Mount Tabor lies east of Nazareth about 2 km off the main Afula to Tiberias road. It is possible to climb to the top via a steep footpath from the village of Dabburiyah on its western face. There is also a rather rough road, involving 15 sharp hairpin bends, rising from the car and coach park at the foot of its north face. Taxis can be hired from this point.

1. *From Nazareth*
Approximately 28 km to the car park. After 11 km, on approaching the outskirts of Afula, turn left at the traffic lights then keep to the left heading towards Tiberias. In a further 12 km take the road on the left towards the mountain. The car park is about 5 km from this point. Circumvent the mount on its west face, motoring through Dabburiyah, until reaching the parking place.

2. *From Tiberias*
Approximately 30 km to the car park. Leave on the main road heading west out of the town and in 15 km turn left at the Golani Junction traffic lights. In a further 10 km pass

through the outskirts of Kfar Tavor and then, in about 1½ km take the turning on the right, at the bottom of the hill, signposted 'Mount Tabor'. The parking place is about 3½ km from this point.

History

The mountain has played an important part in the history of the land since very early times because of its strategic position on the main trade route between East and West. Many battles have been fought at its foot in the plain of Jezreel (also known as Esdraelon). As early as 2000 BC the Caananites set up a place of worship to Baal on its summit. In Psalm 89 we read: 'Tabor and Hermon shall rejoice in the name of the Lord'. During the time of the Judges, Deborah the Prophetess and Barak the General assembled their armies here to rout the Caananite chariots of Sisera. The arab village of Dabburiyah at its western foot is still named after the Prophetess. There is also a tradition that Jesus healed the epileptic boy in this village.

In the sixth century the Anonymous Pilgrim of Piacenza records that there were three churches on the Mount. These were later destroyed by the Persians in AD 614. In 1099 Tancred, the Crusader Knight, built a fortress and a monastery which was occupied by the Benedictine Monks until the

defeat of the Crusader Kingdom in 1187. In the thirteenth century the Saracens constructed a defensive wall with twelve watchtowers around the summit.

Tour

At the top of the twisting ascent road is a stone archway, appropriately named the 'Gate of the Winds'. There was once a drawbridge here and to the right can be seen remnants of a wall built by Flavius Josephus in the first century AD. Continue along the driveway towards the Franciscan Church. Through the trees, on the left, can be seen the small red dome of the Greek Orthodox Church which was built in 1911 on Crusader and Byzantine remains. It is dedicated to the prophet Elijah and contains some fine ikons and mosaics although unfortunately the church is often closed to visitors. Ahead on the right is a public car park, while further on taxis unload their passengers in front of the wrought iron gates leading to the Franciscan Church.

Within the gates the path is flanked by the ruins of the twelfth century Benedictine Monastery which itself was built upon earlier Byzantine foundations. Notice halfway along on the left of the path the outline of a small chapel, clearly identified by its eastern apse, which dates from the sixth century and was later adapted for use by the Crusaders. On both sides of the path can be seen other remains of the Benedictine Monastery including, on the left, the central hall and the refectory.

The present church was erected in 1924 by Spanish Franciscans and is one of the largest in the Holy Land – a major achievement bearing in mind that all the building material had to be carried to the top of the mountain. The style is typical of Byzantine basilicas. The Italian architect was Antonio Barluzzi who designed many of the churches built in the Holy Land this century. A bronze bas-relief commemorating his life is set into the wall opposite the west door.

The interior of the Church is most impressive and an unusual feature is that the nave is at a middle level between the main altar and the crypt. Notice the fine mosaic on the oven vaulting of the apse depicting Our Lord's Transfiguration. On the left is St Peter, while on the right are St James and St John. In the background, standing upon clouds, are Moses and the Prophet Elijah. The open crypt below is full of colour and is greatly enhanced by the brilliant stained glass east window depicting two peacocks (symbols of eternity) flanking a chalice. The plain stone blocks of the Crusader altar, and the three lower courses of the apse from the same period, fittingly complement the modern decorations. In the floor in front of the altar, below wooden trapdoors, are Byzantine and Caananite remains.

Before leaving the church visit the two chapels under the west towers. The one on the north side is dedicated to Moses who is portrayed in a painting inside, directly above the entrance door. In a similar position in the other chapel on the south side, dedicated to Elijah, is a painting of this Prophet.

On leaving the Church turn immediately left and ascend a flight of steps onto a higher level. From here there is a magnificent view across the plain of Jezreel which today is regarded as the 'Breadbasket of Israel'. Notice how some fields are being sown, some reaped and others ploughed. The ground is so fertile that it is possible to grow three crops each year. On the horizon are the Gilboa Mountains of King Saul fame, whilst on the left is the village of Endor where he consulted the witch as related in I Samuel 28.7. Look half right and notice, beyond the main road, the village of Nain where Jesus brought to life again the only son of a widow.

Return to the wrought iron gates. On the left is the Franciscan Monastery and Convent where the nuns sometimes offer for sale a small selection of souvenirs.

Authors' Comments

Although the Gospels do not specify where the Transfiguration took place – and modern scholars now feel that the much higher Mount Hermon is a more likely location – Tabor is nevertheless the only mountain upon which churches have been erected to commemorate the event. Quite apart from the magnificent views from the summit, it is surrounded in mystique and atmosphere. In particular it should be seen in the early morning from the main Tiberias to Afula road when sometimes, and quite suddenly, low cloud hides the summit from sight just as described in the Gospel story.

Opening Times:
8.00–12.00 14.00–18.00
(Winter closes 17.00)
Closed on Saturday

Souvenir Shop: A small selection of gifts in the refectory

Toilets: Near the car park and on the right of the entrance inside the refectory

Custodians: The Church of the Transfiguration: Franciscans
The Church of Elijah: Greek Orthodox

Telephone: (06) 767489 (Franciscan Monastery).

The Transfiguration (Luke 9. 28–36)

Jesus took Peter, John, and James and went up a mountain to pray. And while he was praying the appearance of his face changed and his clothes became dazzling white. Suddenly there were two men talking with him – Moses and Elijah – who appeared in glory and spoke of his departure, the destiny he was to fulfil in Jerusalem. Peter and his companions had been overcome by sleep; but when they awoke, they saw his glory and the two men who stood beside him. As these two were moving away from Jesus, Peter said to him, 'Master, it is good that we are here. Shall we make three shelters, one for you, one for Moses, and one for Elijah?' but he spoke without knowing what he was saying. As he spoke there came a cloud which cast its shadow over them; they were afraid as they entered the cloud, and from it a voice spoke: 'This is my Son, my Chosen; listen to him.' After the voice had spoken, Jesus was seen to be alone. The disciples kept silence and did not at that time say a word to anyone of what they had seen. (REB)

'Tis good, Lord, to be here,
Yet we may not remain;
but since thou bidst us leave the mount,
come with us to the plain.'

For further Gospel references, see page 198

Cana

Since early Christian times many have believed that this Arab village of Kafr Kanna is where Jesus performed his first miracle by turning water into wine at a wedding feast. There were Byzantine and Crusader churches here although the present Roman Catholic and Greek Orthodox buildings commemorating the event date only from the nineteenth century. Cana was also the home of Nathaniel, an early Disciple of Our Lord.

Access

Kafr Kanna lies north-east of Nazareth on the road to Tiberias. Both churches are situated in the centre of the village about 200 metres off the main road.

1. *From Nazareth:* The village is 11 km from the town. On approaching look for the Kafr Kanna village sign and in a further 800 metres for a domed church on the right. 100 metres beyond this (just past the bus stop) a narrow road leads up to the wedding churches. It is advisable to park at a convenient place on the main road. The Greek Orthodox Church is reached

first in about 100 metres. To visit the Franciscan Church bear right and continue for another 50 metres.

2. *From Tiberias:* The village is 24 km from the town. Take the Tel-Aviv road and in 15 km keep straight ahead at the Golani Junction traffic lights. In a further 7 km turn left, signposted 'Nazareth'. In about 800 metres look out for the Kafr Kanna sign, and in a further 1 km opposite the large electricity transformer, a narrow road leads up to the wedding churches. It is advisable to park at a convenient place on the main road. Walk up to the

Franciscan Church, a distance of about 200 metres. The Greek Orthodox Church is 50 metres further along on the right.

* * *

THE FRANCISCAN CHURCH OF THE WEDDING FEAST

Tour

The present church, easily identified by its two western towers and a red dome, was built in 1879. However there are remains of earlier Crusader and Byzantine buildings in the crypt. Of particular significance is the fact that in the fourth century St Paula and St Eustochium, disciples of St Jerome, recorded in a letter that they: 'Saw Cana, not far from Nazareth, where the water was changed into wine'.

Look round the church. The interior is typical of its period and there is little of particular interest at ground level although an unusual feature is that the eastern end is

The Wedding Feast (John 2. 1–11)

Two days later there was a wedding at Cana-in-Galilee. The mother of Jesus was there, and Jesus and his disciples were also among the guests. The wine gave out, so Jesus's mother said to him, 'They have no wine left.' He answered, 'That is no concern of mine. My hour has not yet come.' His mother said to the servants, 'Do whatever he tells you.' There were six stone water-jars standing near, of the kind used for Jewish rites of purification; each held from twenty to thirty gallons. Jesus said to the servants, 'Fill the jars with water,' and they filled them to the brim. 'Now draw some off,' he ordered, 'and take it to the master of the feast'; and they did so.

The master tasted the water now turned into wine, not knowing its source, though the servants who had drawn the water knew. He hailed the bridegroom and said, 'Everyone else serves the best wine first, and the poorer only when the guests have drunk freely; but you have kept the best wine till now.' So Jesus performed at Cana-in-Galilee the first of the signs which revealed his glory and led his disciples to believe in him. (REB)

'The Gospel story has recorded
how your glory was afforded
to a wedding day;
be our guest, we pray.'

For further Gospel references, see page 195

elevated to accommodate the ancient remains in the crypt below. Before descending into the crypt notice that in the floor nearby, under a metal grille, there is a 3rd/4th century mosaic written in Aramaic. A translation can be found on the south wall: 'Honoured be the memory of Yosef, son of Tanham, son of Buta and his sons who made this, may it be a blessing to them. Amen'.

It is claimed that the inscription was originally part of a synagogue bench and that the Yosef referred to may have been Joseph of Tiberias who was converted to Christianity during the Constantinian period and founded many churches in Galilee.

Descend the stairs into the crypt. In the centre, protected by railings and standing on Byzantine foundations, is a commemorative water pot. Those mentioned in St John's Gospel were much larger and held 20–30 gallons. It should be remembered that it was not unusual for wedding celebrations to last for a whole week.

From a passageway to the right of the altar can be seen the remains of an ancient cistern, while on the left are some more water jars. In a room on the left of the crypt are remnants from Crusader, Byzantine and earlier periods.

Opening Times:
8.00–12.00 14.30–18.00 daily (Winter closes at 17.00)

Souvenir Shop: Opposite the main entrance

Toilets: None

Custodian: The Franciscans

Telephone: (06) 517011

THE GREEK ORTHODOX CHURCH OF THE WEDDING FEAST

Standing within its own compound, the church built in the shape of a Greek cross, is surmounted by a distinctive dome. The interior contains a number of ikons and holy pictures.

Opening Times:
8.30–18.30

N.B. An alternative site for Cana in Galilee is Khirbet Cana which is about 14 km north of Nazareth. Apparently it was favoured in the middle ages although today there is nothing to be seen but a mound of ruins. Certainly Kafr Kanna has more to offer.

Authors' Comments

Aesthetically neither the churches nor the village are particularly attractive. Nevertheless Cana in Galilee has always held a very special place in the affections of those who have been blessed with a happy Christian marriage.

Nazareth

Church of the Annunciation
St Joseph's Church
Church of St Gabriel (Mary's Well)
The Old Synagogue

The words 'Jesus of Nazareth' highlight for Christians the importance of this otherwise relatively insignificant town. There are four places of primary importance: The Basilica of the Annunciation; The Church of St Joseph (the 'Carpenter's Shop'); The Church of St Gabriel ('Mary's Well'); and the Greek Catholic Church built over the traditional site of the Synagogue of Our Lord's time.

THE TOWN

The old town nestles in a valley and should not be confused with Nazareth Ilit, the modern Israeli suburb four kilometres to the east and easily identified by its profusion of tall buildings.

Nazareth is the largest Arab town in northern Israel and the commercial centre for the many surrounding villages. It is a bustling traffic-congested place and in the summer can be both hot and dusty. As in Bethlehem the population is predominantly Christian and there are a number of church schools and religious foundations.

The principal sites should be visited on foot and are all within a fairly small area. Car parking can be difficult, especially on Saturday when there is a market. The modern Basilica of the Annunciation is in the centre of the town and its cupola surmounted by a lantern is the distinctive feature.

THE BASILICA OF THE ANNUNCIATION

This imposing modern Basilica was erected over what is claimed to be part of the home of the Blessed Virgin Mary and is the fifth building for Christian worship on this site. Funded by Roman Catholic communities throughout the world, work commenced in 1955 on the largest church erected in the Holy Land for nearly 800 years. It was completed in 1969.

Tour

From inside the entrance gates stop to view the west facade which is dedicated to the Mystery of the Incarnation. At the apex is a statue of Jesus and immediately below, in bas-relief, is depicted the angel of the Lord bringing the news to Mary, with the appropriate inscription in Latin underneath. Below are the four Evangelists – Matthew, Mark, Luke and John – with their traditional symbols: man, lion, bull and eagle. To the left is part of a quotation from Genesis 3.14–15: 'The Lord God said unto the serpent . . . And I will put emnity between

thee and the woman, and between thy seed and her seed; it shall bruise thy head, and thou shall bruise his heel'. To the right is another quotation from Isaiah 7.14: 'Behold, a virgin shall conceive, and bear a son, and shall call his name Immanuel'. Finally, above the triple doorway is a quotation from John 1.14: 'The Word was made flesh, and dwelt among us'.

Before entering the Church turn right to see the colourful wall mosaics along the cloisters which are gifts from Roman Catholic communities throughout the world. The one nearest the entrance gate commemorates the visit of Pope Paul VI to the town in January 1964.

While standing on this side of the Basilica stop to view the south facade across which are inscribed the words of the Roman Catholic devotion 'Salve Regina'. In the centre above the doorway is a bronze statue of the young Mary extending a welcome to all who come into her house. On the door, depicted in bronze, are twelve scenes from the life of the Blessed Virgin.

Return to the west facade and look at the three doors. On the massive central door, boldly depicted in bronze, are six events in the life of Christ. Viewing them anti-clockwise from the top left, they are: the Nativity in Bethlehem; the flight into Egypt; life in the

Carpenter's shop here in Nazareth; Baptism in the River Jordan; teaching by the Galilean lakeside; and The Crucifixion. In addition to these central portrayals are also depicted in copper ten other incidents recorded in the Gospels. Turning to the door on the left, the scenes here show the fall of man and its consequences. The door on the right depicts three prophesies of redemption from the books of the Old Testament: 2 Samuel 7.16; Isaiah 7.14; Ezekiel 9.4.

Now enter the Basilica. It has two levels and this is the lower Church. Walk across to the balustrade surrounding the most sacred area which is three metres below the modern floor. The main feature is the remains of an exposed cavern venerated as the place where the angel Gabriel appeared to Mary. Move round to stand in a position directly opposite this Grotto of the Annunciation. It is flanked by the remnants of earlier Byzantine and Crusader churches. The four metre high wall constructed of columns and large stone blocks which acts as a backdrop to this scene also formed part of the Crusaders' building. The altar within the grotto is from the Franciscan Church built on a fairly modest scale in 1730, enlarged in 1877, and finally demolished in 1954 to make way for the present Basilica.

Lean over the balustrade to discern immediately below two parallel strips of mosaic. The one nearest the railings could possibly have been part of the floor of the earliest known religious building on this site – a 2nd/3rd century 'Synagogue-Church'. The other dates from the fifth century, and on the right can clearly be seen two remaining wall-courses from the apse of this Byzantine Church. Before leaving the area look up at an octagonal opening which affords a view of this venerated site from the Upper Church.

Returning towards the entrance, ascend the spiral staircase on the left passing the brilliantly coloured windows of encrusted glass. The steps lead to the upper floor which serves as the Parish Church for the Roman Catholic community in Nazareth.

Walk down the right aisle to view on the south wall the impressive decorative panels. These adorn both aisles and are gifts from twenty countries. They portray in a variety of materials the veneration of the Blessed Virgin. Now turn to notice the fine stained glass window at the back of the nave.

Stand centrally in front of the railings, facing the High Altar, and look up to the magnificent cupola 55 metres high and 16 metres in circumference. The name Nazareth is a Semitic word which means a flower and the cupola represents an inverted lily rooted in heaven opening its petals to the shrine below to crown the place of the Annunciation.

The Italian mosaic above the altar is one of the largest in the world and portrays Jesus with his arms outstretched beside St Peter surrounded by numerous representatives of Christendom. At Our Lord's right hand is the crowned Virgin seated in glory, while overhead is the dove of the Holy Spirit and the all-seeing eye of the Father.

The chapel to the left of the high altar is dedicated to St Francis, whilst the one to the right is consecrated to the Holy Spirit. From this central position it is also of interest to note that the full length wall

---

The Annunciation (Luke 1. 26–38)

And in the sixth month the angel Gabriel was sent from God, unto a city of Galilee, named Nazareth, to a virgin espoused to a man whose name was Joseph, of the house of David; and the virgin's name was Mary. And the angel came in unto her, and said, 'Hail, thou that art highly favoured, the Lord is with thee: blessed art thou among women'. And when she saw him, she was troubled at his saying, and cast in her mind what manner of salutation this should be. And the angel said unto her, 'Fear not, Mary: for thou hast found favour with God. And, behold, thou shalt conceive in thy womb, and bring forth a son, and shalt call his name JESUS. He shall be great, and shall be called the Son of the Highest: and the Lord God shall give unto him the throne of his father David: and he shall reign over the House of Jacob for ever; and of his kingdom there shall be no end'.

Then said Mary unto the angel, 'How shall this be, seeing I know not a man?' And the angel answered and said unto her, 'The Holy Ghost shall come upon thee, and the power of the Highest shall overshadow thee; therefore also that holy thing which shall be born of thee shall be called the Son of God. And, behold, thy cousin Elizabeth, she hath also conceived a son in her old age: and this is the sixth month with her who was called barren. For with God nothing shall be impossible'. And Mary said, 'Behold the handmaid of the Lord; be it unto me according to thy word'. And the angel departed from her. (AV)

'Love divine, all loves excelling,
joy of heaven, to earth come down,
fix in us thy humble dwelling,
all thy faithful mercies crown.'

For further Gospel references, see page 197

mosaic nearest to the Franciscan chapel is a gift from England and depicts Our Lady of Walsingham. The 'Slipper Chapel' is featured in the mosaic.

Observe the other plaques on the north wall and then leave the building through the door on this side. Ahead is the Baptistry which, in accordance with an early Christian custom, is separated from the main building because the un-baptised were not allowed to enter the church. The panels of amethyst and green glass represent the flowing baptismal water. The font itself is cast in bronze and on it can be seen a modern representation of Jesus being baptised by John. This entire structure was a gift from Germany.

On the north side of the Baptistry, and well below the level of the present courtyard, can be seen some of the passages, stores, silos and water cisterns which existed under the simple dwellings of Our Lord's time. Here one is looking on features which were familiar to Jesus and his family. This system of underground caverns is a continuation of the Grotto of the Annunciation. Further examples are also visible in the crypt of St Joseph's Church, the next place to visit.

Before leaving this particular area turn back to view the impressive cupola of the

Basilica which is topped by a lantern symbolising the Light of the World.

Opening Times:
Summer: 8.30–12.00 14.00–17.45
Sundays: afternoons only 14.00–17.30
Winter: closes daily at 16.30
Sundays: afternoons only 14.00–16.30

Souvenir Shop: None

Toilets: Inside the main gates and turn to the left

Custodian: The Franciscans

Telephone: (06) 572501

*　　*　　*

ST JOSEPH'S CHURCH
THE CHURCH OF THE CARPENTER'S SHOP

Access

From the Church of the Annunciation ascend the steps beyond the Baptistry and turn right. Ahead is the main entrance to the Franciscan Monastery built in 1930. On the second floor is the Terra Sancta High School which provides education for about 700 pupils. On the lawn in front of the Monastery are remains from the four earlier churches. Continue past the main entrance and ascend further steps leading to St Joseph's Church also known as the 'Church of the Carpenter's Shop'. Turn left at the top and enter by the west door because the other in the south wall is used as an exit.

Tour

This Church built in 1914 follows the line of an earlier Crusader building the foundations of which were discovered in 1895. Now proceed to the aisle on the left and before descending the stairway into the crypt notice the well known painting by the French artist Francois Lafond on the north wall.

There are five main features in the crypt. Stand in front of the altar and notice the eight stone courses of the apse which remain from the crusader building. In the floor, slightly to the left, is a metal grille through which there is a view of the caverns below. These probably date from about 1000 BC. Originally they were grain silos but later were adapted as living accommodation and were used for domestic purposes until the end of the last century. Next move to the back of the crypt and look over the wrought iron guard to view a pit about three metres square with a mosaic floor and seven steps leading down to it. The Franciscans claim this was a Baptismal pool dating from the Judeo-Christian era circa 1st–3rd century AD.

Leave the crypt by the other side. On ascending the stairway, notice on the right a further flight of ancient steps leading down to the complex of caverns underneath the whole area. On the left of the stairway can also be seen an old water cistern. Leave the Church by the south door. The exit from the compound is opposite the main entrance to the Monastery.

Opening Times:
See the Church of the Annunciation

Souvenir Shop:
A small booth beside the Church

Toilets: See the Church of the Annunciation

Custodian:
The Franciscans

Telephone: (06) 572501

*   *   *

Authors' Comments

No one can really be certain of the exact location of the home of the Holy Family or of the Carpenter's Shop. It is hardly surprising that today nothing remains of the simple houses that Jesus knew, but there is ample evidence that these two Christian sites have been venerated from an early period. The caverns hewn out of the bedrock below the dwellings are clearly visible and undoubtedly some would have been used for domestic purposes because they were warm in winter and cool in summer. This area owned by the Franciscans makes a pleasing haven from the hustle and bustle outside and here there are many opportunities for devotion and reflection.

THE CHURCH OF ST GABRIEL

THE CHURCH OF MARY'S WELL

The Church is built over the only fresh-water spring in Nazareth and would have been visited daily by the Holy Family.

Access

1. From the exit of the Franciscan compound of the Church of the Annunciation and St Joseph's Church turn immediately right and follow the boundary wall around. Then keep straight ahead for about 450 metres until reaching the Church of St Gabriel.

2. When approaching Nazareth from Tiberias it is better to call here first before proceeding to the Church of the Annunciation. On completing the steep and twisty descent into the Arab town, look out on the right for the solid-looking modern stone structure with a circular recess facing the main road. This is known as 'Mary's Well' and until fairly recently was a public wash-house. St Gabriel's Church is about 75 metres behind it.

Tour

St Gabriel's is surrounded by a high wall and is approached through a central gateway. Walk across the courtyard and descend the steps under the portico which lead directly into the south aisle of this Greek Orthodox Church. However before examining it in detail, continue straight ahead and descend further steps into a low vaulted cavern built by the Crusaders in the twelfth century.

At the end is a metal balustrade below which can be seen the clear spring water. It is not possible to date this particular outlet of the spring, but certainly the Holy Family and the inhabitants of

Nazareth depended upon its waters 2,000 years ago. The Greek Orthodox believe that the Archangel Gabriel first appeared to Mary at the spring as related in the Apocryphal Gospel of St James.

Before returning to look around the Church, notice the ancient Armenian tiles with which the Crusaders decorated the walls. There is a small recess in the wall with a shaft where it is possible to let down a metal cup and draw up the water.

Now move up to view the Church which was built in 1769. The walls and ceiling are lavishly decorated with modern murals. The main altar is hidden from view by a screen known as the 'iconostasis' which is decorated with icons and other holy pictures. Within the nave on the right is the Bishop's throne while high up on the left is the tall pulpit. Against the north wall can be seen the tomb of the founder of the Church.

Opening Times:
Summer: 8.00–11.45 15.00–18.00 daily
(Winter: closes at 17.30)

Toilets: Within the courtyard

Custodian: The Greek Orthodox Church. A small donation is expected in the box by the door

Telephone: (06) 574566

Authors' Comments

There is no doubt about the authenticity of this fresh water spring and with a little imagination one can picture a small boy coming to draw water – perhaps twice daily – with his young mother.

*   *   *

THE OLD SYNAGOGUE

There is a tradition that this simple building stands on the site of the synagogue of Our Lord's time.

Access

From the exit of the Franciscan compound of the Church of the Annunciation and St Joseph's Church, walk down the road opposite the gates for about 100 metres and then turn up to the right into the paved shopping mall. Keep ascending along this street turning first to the left, then to the right. After that in about 20 metres, on the right, look out for a doorway by the remains of an ancient pillar (ring the bell if the door is closed) and enter a small courtyard which leads into the Old Synagogue.

Details

The interior of this little Crusader building, owned by the Greek Catholic Church, is devoid of any furniture except for a few wooden stalls around the walls and the plain altar at the end. It is claimed that the floor dates from a much earlier period.

Nazareth

Authors' Comments

This is an appropriate place in which to reflect that in the Synagogue at Nazareth Jesus was taught and learned to read. Here he read aloud the scriptures – and here he proclaimed their fulfilment.

Opening Times:
8.30–18.00 daily (ring the bell)

Souvenir Shop: None

Toilets: None

Custodian: The Greek Catholic Church
A small donation is expected

Telephone: (06) 568488

*   *   *

If time permits it is well worth ascending the numerous flights of steps to the top of the hill overlooking the town. From here there is a good view over Nazareth. In the middle distance is a hill on which there is a cluster of trees close to a small chapel. This is known as the Mount of Precipitation from which, according to tradition, the Nazarenes intended to throw Jesus down when he was driven out of the City.

Near this viewpoint is the Silesian Secondary School which has a fine chapel dedicated to the Adolescence of Jesus. In a niche high above the altar is an impressive statue depicting him as a young boy.

While in Nazareth it is also worth exploring the streets in the vicinity of the Old Synagogue because here are a number of modern carpenters' shops.

Teaching in the Synagogue (Luke 4. 16–21)

Jesus came to Nazareth, where he had been brought up, and went to the synagogue on the sabbath day as he regularly did. He stood up to read the lesson and was handed the scroll of the prophet Isaiah. He opened the scroll and found the passage which says, 'The spirit of the Lord is upon me because he has anointed me; he has sent me to announce good news to the poor, to proclaim release for prisoners and recovery of sight for the blind; to let the broken victims go free, to proclaim the year of the Lord's favour.' He rolled up the scroll, gave it back to the attendant, and sat down; and all eyes in the synagogue were fixed on him. He began to address them: 'Today, he said, 'In your hearing this text has come true.' (REB)

> 'Lord, thy word abideth,
> and our footsteps guideth;
> who its truth believeth
> light and joy receiveth.'

For further Gospel references, see page 197

Acre

Situated on the northern sweep of the Bay of Haifa, this picturesque walled town with its fishing harbour gives the impression today of being entirely medieval. In fact, most of it was rebuilt at the end of the eighteenth century having been totally destroyed on the defeat of the Crusaders in 1291. It is they, who in less than two centuries, left the greatest impression upon its long and chequered history. Within the walls are the substantial remains of their Head-quarters – often referred to as the 'Underground City'. Also of particular interest are three merchants' khans (trading stations), a network of narrow streets and the impressive Mosque of Ahmed el-Jazzar.

Access

Acre (spelt on some maps as Akko, or Acco) by road is 22 km north of Haifa, 56 km from Tiberias and 181 km from Jerusalem. Although the skyline of the Old City can clearly be seen from the coastal road when driving from the south, it is not visible when approaching from the east (Tiberias or Safed). In both instances it is first necessary to drive through the modern town to reach the Old City.

1. *From Tiberias*: On reaching the outskirts of Acre keep straight on at the first two traffic lights. Immediately beyond the second light, on the left, is a large mound (tel) which is the site of the ancient city. Soon after this is a railway level crossing, and then shortly afterwards at the roundabout keep straight ahead towards the centre of

the town until reaching the pedestrian precinct. Here turn right. Take the first left, then proceed over the first crossroads and turn left at the second. Drive through two further crossroads then keep straight on to pass through the Crusader defensive walls. Look out for the parking signs to the left. From the car park entrance the slim round minaret and dome of the Mosque of El-Jazzar where our tour commences are clearly visible.

2. *From Haifa*: On approaching Acre at the northern end of Haifa Bay look out on the left for the Palm Beach Hotel and at the roundabout turn immediately right. In 800 metres turn left at the next roundabout towards the centre of the town until reaching the pedestrian precinct. Here turn right. Take the first left, then proceed over the first crossroads and turn left at the second. Drive through two further crossroads then keep straight on to pass through the Crusader defensive walls. Look out for the parking signs to the left. From the car park entrance the slim round minaret and dome of the Mosque of El-Jazzar where our tour commences are clearly visible.

History

The large mound (tel) marking the site of the ancient city is 1½ km inland and is one of the oldest recorded settlements in the Holy Land. It was an important Canaanite city long before being mentioned in Egyptian writings of the eighteenth century BC. At the time of David and Solomon, around 1000 BC, it was a substantial Phoenician town under the control of Tyre, but little is known about its development during this period because it lay outside ancient Israel.

During the reign of Alexander the Great (356–323 BC) the town was of particular importance and even had its own mint which remained in use for a further six hundred years. In the middle of the third century BC Acre came under the rule of the Ptolemies of Egypt. The city was renamed Ptolemais after that dynasty, its prosperity grew even further, and the inhabitants spread beyond the bounds of the ancient mound towards the sea.

During the Roman period, from 63 BC, a colony was established within its walls for war veterans and Julius Caesar himself visited in 47 BC.

St Paul spent a day with the Christian community in Ptolemais on returning from his third missionary journey (Acts 21.7). By AD 190 Acre had its first Bishop. Byzantine influence remained until 636 when the Arabs captured the city and further developed the harbour.

Acre's heyday was during the historical period known as 'The Crusades'. In AD 1095 Pope Urban II in response to an appeal from the Emperor of Constantinople, persuaded some of the more powerful nations in Europe to recruit armies to rescue the Eastern Christians from the Muslims. The Pope's ultimate objective was to free the Holy Land, and in particular the Tomb of Christ, from Islamic control. Thousands enthusiastically took up such a worthwhile cause and it was thought that the campaign would be relatively short-lived. Jerusalem was captured in 1099 and Acre fell in 1104 when it was immediately used by the Crusaders for the landing of vital supplies and arms. The port also became an important trading link between the West and the East because its natural harbour was one of the best on the Eastern Mediterranean coast.

During the early part of the twelfth century two great military Orders were founded. The first, the chivalrous 'Hospitallers of St John of Jerusalem' concerned themselves with the health and spiritual well-being of pilgrims. They built their substantial headquarters in Acre. Much of this known as 'The Underground City' can still be seen today. (Details follow under 'Tour'). They also founded a number of hospitals and built a Cathedral on the site now occupied by El-Jazzar's Mosque.

The second Order of Knights, 'The Templars', were responsible for the defence of Jerusalem and they used the El Aqsa Mosque on the Temple Mount as their headquarters. The Crusaders also set about an ambitious building programme restoring Acre's city walls. At that time the area enclosed was three times larger than it is now.

One of the inherent weaknesses of the Crusades was that they lacked overall command and the various armies pursued their own objectives. In Acre itself rich merchants from the Italian City States such as Genoa, Pisa and Venice developed their separate quarters but much rivalry soon grew between them.

There was also some discord amongst the knights of the nations involved, and these factors undoubtedly contributed to the eventual downfall of the 'Latin Kingdom', as it was then known because the Mass and other Offices of the Church were in latin. Even today the Roman Catholic Community in the Holy Land is known by the Eastern Churches as the 'Latins'.

In 1187 Saladin defeated the Crusaders at the Horns of Hattin and Acre subsequently was taken, but it was recaptured only four years later by soldiers under the command of King Philip of France and the King of England Richard 'the Lionheart'.

In 1219 following a decision by the General Chapter of the Franciscan Order to extend their mission throughout the world, St Francis of Assisi visited Acre and as a result their first monastery in the East was established. The City remained in Crusader hands as all that was left of the Latin Kingdom until their final expulsion in 1291 by the Egyptian Marmelukes.

In order to ensure that the port was no longer used for trade, Acre was razed to the ground and lay in ruins for the next four hundred and fifty years.

In 1750 during a decadent period of the Ottoman empire an Arab sheikh, Daher el-Omar, created his own kingdom in Galilee and his influence spread as far as the coast. He commenced the redevelopment of Acre as a trading port especially for use between Syria and the western Mediterranean. Daher el-Omar was assassinated in 1775 but was succeeded by an Albanian soldier el-Jazzar, nicknamed 'the Butcher' because of his extreme cruelty. The Turks appointed him Governor of Acre and with great determination he rebuilt the City on the same pattern as that of

Constantinople. Trade once again flourished and amongst his many achievements was the building of one of the finest mosques in Palestine which was named after him. He also restored the walls, erected many public buildings including the three great Khans, and further developed the harbour. Most of the old city buildings seen today date from the period of el-Jazzar.

In 1799 Napoleon, in a bid to extend his eastern empire, laid siege to Acre for two months. However el-Jazzar, assisted by the British fleet under the command of Sir Sydney Smith and with the help of Turkish soldiers from Damascus, forced Napoleon to retreat. This proved to be a turning point in Napoleon's ambitions and consequently he had to abandon any thought of extending his empire as far as India.

Apart from a short period of only eight years from 1832 when Ibrahim Pasha of Egypt drove the Turks out, Acre remained under Turkish control until it fell to the British in 1918. Finally in 1948, at the instigation of the United Nations, Acre came under the jurisdiction of the State of Israel and since then there has been extensive development of the adjacent modern town.

Tour

The Old City should be explored on foot. Our tour

commences at the El-Jazzar Mosque (see 'Access' details from the nearest car park on page 175–6). Because it is so easy to lose one's way in the bewildering network of narrow streets, the following is a suggested route covering most of the features normally included in a guided tour.

El-Jazzar's Mosque

A small entrance fee is payable to the custodian at the gate. Built by el-Jazzar in 1781 it is one of the most attractive mosques in Israel and its pleasant courtyard provides an oasis of tranquillity from the bustle outside. The slender minaret and much of the interior had to be reconstructed at the end of the nineteenth century following an earthquake.

In the centre of the courtyard stands a ritual cleansing fountain. The entire area is surrounded by a colonnaded cloister behind which are small rooms designed for use by Muslim students and pilgrims. Most of the granite and marble columns, together with those in the Mosque itself are Roman and date from the first century BC. They were removed from Caesarea 50 km further down the coast. To the right of the Mosque is a small mausoleum containing the tombs of Ahmed el-Jazzar and his successor Suleiman Pasha.

Beneath the courtyard is the original crypt of the Crusader Cathedral which once stood on this site. It is now used as a water cistern and a flight of steps giving access to it can be found in the far left-hand corner of the courtyard diagonally across from the street entrance.

The interior of the Mosque is of typical Muslim design which tourists are allowed only to view from just inside the main entrance. Ahead in the far wall is a niche known as a 'mihrab' indicating the direction of Mecca towards which worshippers are required to face. To the right of this is the pulpit with steps leading up to it from the front. The area beneath the balcony on the right is reserved for Muslim women, as is the balcony itself where they are segregated from the men. Notice the strings running across the Persian carpets to assist the men in lining up for public worship.

Crusader Headquarters

The extensive remains of the twelfth century Headquarters of the Knights Hospitallers are sometimes referred to as the **Underground City** because today they lie well below street level.

The entrance and ticket booth is opposite El-Jazzar's Mosque. The walls of the courtyard beyond the ticket booth bear witness to the substantial way in which the European Knights constructed their buildings. At the far end is the entrance to the **Knights' Halls**. Originally there were seven and each was occupied by the Knights from different parts of Europe: England, France, Germany, Italy, Spain, Provence and Auvergne.

From here follow the directions to the **Knights' Refectory**. This crypt-like hall with its three massive pillars supporting the vaulted ceiling is one of the finest examples of thirteenth century Crusader architecture. The ground has been excavated around the base of the third pillar to reveal a 'secret' tunnel which was discovered by the Crusaders during their building work. Archaeologists now consider it was originally a sewer dating back to well before the birth of Christ. The Knights further developed it for use as a communicating passage and it is thought that other sections, yet to be excavated, may reach as far as the sea.

Walk through the 100 metre long tunnel which is narrow and in places the roof is rather low, but lighting has been installed. The tunnel eventually leads out into further sections of the Crusader headquarters where there are more vaulted ceilings. The area immediately ahead was probably used as their hospital. On the way out into the daylight notice on either side of the passageway inscribed stones which have

been removed from Crusader tombs.

Mount the wooden stairway, completing the tour of 'the Underground City', turn right at the top, and then shortly right again, into a long covered passageway where there are a few craft shops. Follow the passageway towards the daylight and when outside turn left.

Route to the Khan El-Umdan and the Harbour

In 70 metres there is a large open space. Cross this keeping to the left and in the far left-hand corner turn to the left. Within 10 metres turn right, descend the steps, and then turn right again into a covered street with shops on either side. Walk along this street for 100 metres and at the end turn left. Continue ahead for 40 metres then turn right to reach another open area. Proceed towards the harbour, but divert to the right to walk under a five-storeyed tower which leads into the **Khan el-Umdan** (Inn of Pillars) commonly known as the **Camel Market**, although camels are no longer traded here. On all four sides are granite columns which were removed from Caesarea by Ahmed el-Jazzar when in 1785 he rebuilt this merchants' inn. The Khan originally belonged to the City State of Genoa. Notice the large octagonal trough in the centre of the courtyard.

Return to the entrance and turn immediately right to walk to the picturesque fishing harbour where there is much to see.

If time is not at a premium it is well worth walking along the southern walls beyond the harbour. For the more adventurous there are also two other khans and several churches to explore, but a map is essential.

Opening Times:
El-Jazzar's Mosque
No admission during Muslim times of prayer.

Crusader Headquarters ('Underground City')
June 16th–September 14th: 9.00–18.00. Fridays closes 13.00
September 15th–June 15th: 9.00–17.00. Fridays closes 13.00

Souvenir Shop: None

Toilets: Almost opposite the Knights' Halls

Custodian: The Old Acre Development Company

Khan el-Umdan
Always open

Megiddo

An archaeological site of extreme antiquity which occupied a strategic position on the south-western edge of the Plain of Jezreel commanding the trade routes between Egypt in the south, Asia Minor in the north and Babylon in the East. Within the impressive mound (tel) twenty stratas of man's habitation have been revealed. The site fell into disuse four hundred years before the birth of Christ.

Through the centuries so many bloody battles had been fought on the Plain that the name 'Armageddon' (a corruption of the Hebrew for Hill of Megiddo) came to symbolise the battle to end all battles – the final conflict between good and evil as foretold in the Revelation of St John the Divine: 16.16.

Access

Megiddo lies 35 km south-east of Haifa just north of the intersection of routes 65 and 66. 36 km from Caesarea and 51 km from Tiberias.

A tour of the tel itself as suggested below, including the detour, can be completed in about an hour, but allow a little extra time to visit the Museum room.

History

Megiddo dates from about 4000 BC during the Neolithic period (late Stone Age) when its earliest inhabitants lived in caves hewn out of the bedrock. A thousand years later the first of a series of Canaanite cities was built on the site. Among the discoveries from this period is a large circular pagan altar dating from 2800 BC and part of a defensive wall three metres wide and four metres high.

In 1468 BC Pharaoh Thutmosis III, after a great battle with the Canaanite Kings, overran the City. It remained under Egyptian control for the next three centuries and significant finds from this period include hoards of beautifully carved ivory, gold and jewellery.

One of its most prosperous eras was during the reign of King Solomon (965–928 BC). Megiddo is often referred to as 'Solomon's Chariot City', although archaeologists now attribute this particular development to King Ahab (c. 875–854 BC) who constructed stables to accommodate more than 450 horses. It was Ahab who introduced into Israel the worship of the Phoenician god Baal thus provoking the hostility of Elijah and the prophets. The impressive tunnel at the western side of the mound through which water was brought from a spring outside the walls, was also cut during this period. It was the City's lifeline in times of siege.

The battles on the plain of Jezreel (Esdraelon) are far too numerous to list here, but some are described in the Old Testament. During its turbulent history the City was destroyed and rebuilt by its conquerors many times. Foreign invading armies which passed its walls included Canaanites, Egyptians, Israelites, Philistines, Assyrians, Greeks, Romans, Persians, Turks and finally the British in 1917 during the First World War. Field Marshal Allenby set up his headquarters at Megiddo to defeat the Turks and thus secured for himself the title of Viscount Allenby of Megiddo and Felixstowe!

A major archaeological excavation took place between 1925 and 1939 under the auspices of the University of Chicago when a deep trench was cut into the eastern face of the tel exposing over twenty layers of civilisation including the 5000 year-old Canaanite altar. A further series of short investigations were carried out by the late Israeli Professor Yigael Yadin between 1960 and 1972.

Tour

Before commencing the tour a few minutes spent in the small Museum to the right of the entrance with its excellent displays explaining the history of Megiddo is well worthwhile. In a room beyond is a working model of the tel at the time of Solomon.

From the gift shop and cafeteria take the path towards the tel and follow the direction signs to the right at its foot. Notice on the left a flight of perfectly preserved steps nearly 3000 years old which led up to the City gate. Continue ascending the path and pass through the remains of an even older Canaanite triple gateway. Ascend the wooden stairway and notice on the right the remains of a quadruple gateway dating from the time of King Solomon.

Throughout the tel the various features are well marked and do not therefore require a detailed explanation here. Continue the tour by following the arrows until reaching the sign to the 'Northern Observation Platform'.

Proceed to the platform which has two separate viewing positions. The first looks out over the Plain of Jezreel, and against the railings is an orientation plan identifying the main panoramic features. The second overlooks the deep channel cut through the tel during the 1925–39 excavations. The main feature here is the large circular Canaanite altar built of unhewn stones nearly 5000 years ago with seven steps leading up to it. The archaeologists uncovered evidence of four temples in this vicinity, one was several centuries earlier than the altar itself. It is thought that by 1800 BC the temples no longer existed.

Retrace your steps to the main path and turn left to reach the grain silo. It is over seven metres deep and is thought to date from the time of King Jeroboam II (793–753 BC). Round the inside are two stairways which allowed the grain to be collected at separate points. In King Solomon's time there was a palace beyond the silo. The path to the left leads to the far end of the tel from which there is a different view of the Canaanite altar and sacred area from the opposite side of the archaeological cut. Close by can also be seen the ruins of the residence of King Ahab's chariot commander. If taking this detour, return to the silo to resume the tour.

Continue along the main path, bearing round to the left, and make a short diversion to view the remains of the stables built by King Ahab for his 450 chariot horses, but still often incorrectly attributed to King Solomon. In this area can be seen a number of feeding-troughs, a few still with their tethering posts. Some scholars are of the opinion that the stables were in fact storehouses (as at Masada) and that the troughs were for feeding smaller beasts of burden which brought in supplies. Professor Yadin was however convinced that they were designed for chariot horses.

Return to the path and continue towards the underground water system. Originally the inhabitants on the mound depended for their water supply upon an ancient spring which welled-up within a cavern at the foot of the tel. This rendered them vulnerable in times of siege. To overcome the hazard, an ambitious tunnelling project was devised to enable water to be brought safely into the City by an underground route. The work was probably started during Solomon's reign but was certainly completed by Ahab.

It is interesting to note that the Megiddo undertaking was carried out 150 years before Hezekiah quarried his water-tunnel in Jerusalem, and the 70-metre long tunnel here is very much wider in comparison. The descent to it is now via 183 steep steps. Considering its antiquity, it is an incredible feat of engineering. After sinking a shaft thirty metres deep, the task of cutting horizontally through the bedrock was begun from either end and the two gangs of labourers had only to make a small correction to meet in the middle. At the far end of the three metre high tunnel is the original spring, but now in summer the cavern is often quite dry. From here a further 80 steps lead up to a position outside the walls. This opening was sealed on completion of the tunnel so that invaders could not use it to enter the City.

N.B. Unless arrangements have been made to be picked up in the car park near this exit, return through the tunnel and across the tel to the main entrance.

Opening Times:
April to September: 8.00–17.00
October to March: 8.00–16.00
On eve of Shabbat and holidays closes 1 hour earlier. Closed on Yom Kippur. The tourist 'green card' is accepted

Souvenir Shop: Behind the reception area and Museum. Help-yourself snacks and meals available

Toilets: Beside the refreshment area

Custodian: The National Parks Authority

Telephone: (06) 522105

Caesarea

The extensive ruins of this once substantial Mediterranean seaport provide some idea of its size and importance in Our Lord's time. Caesarea was the Provincial Headquarters of the Roman administration and it was here that the Procurator, Pontius Pilate, had his residence. For the Christian it is of great significance because in this city St Peter baptised the first Gentile convert Cornelius, a centurion in the Roman Army. Here, at the home of Philip the Evangelist, Agabus foretold the treatment which St Paul would receive in Jerusalem. Before his trial in Rome Paul himself was imprisoned in Caesarea for two years.

The main sites are: (1) A Roman Theatre restored to seat a twentieth century audience of four thousand. (2) Crusader walled town with its harbour and modern bathing beach. (3) The Roman Aqueduct.

Access

Caesarea is 50 km north of Tel-Aviv and 35 km south of Haifa. It is not prominently marked on some maps because much of the site consists of historical ruins.

1. *From Tel-Aviv*: Take the coastal motorway (Route 2) running north and in about 45 km opposite the huge power station on the left look out for a sign to Afula and Caesarea. Here turn off and then proceed left under the motorway. At the first junction turn right, and on reaching the first roundabout keep straight ahead. At the second roundabout exit left following the signs to the 'Old City' and 'Theatre' until arriving at the coach/car park in front of the ruins of the Roman Theatre (details on page 192).

To visit the Crusader walled town continue along the road running parallel to the sea for about 1 km (passing the coach/car park and the defensive walls on the left) until arriving at another

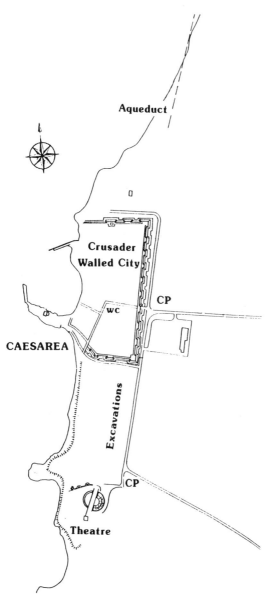

coach/car park straight ahead. (Tour details on page 189).

To reach the Roman Aqueduct drive inland and then in about 1 km take the first road off to the left. In 200 metres turn left again and follow the 'Cluster 2' signs to the Aqueduct. (Details on page 191).

2. *From Haifa*: Drive down Route 2 for about 28 km until reaching the Zikhron Ya'aqov interchange. Here turn off to drive inland for 3 km and join the smaller coastal road (Route 4) running south and signed Zikhron Ya'aqov. Continue towards Tel-Aviv and after 10 km keep a sharp look out on the right for a turning to Caesarea. Drive on this road for 2¼ km keeping straight ahead at a roundabout and then passing under the motorway. Shortly afterwards take the turning off to the right by a modern sculpture. After a further 200 metres turn left at the 'Cluster 2' signs to reach the Aqueduct. (Details on page 191).

In order to reach the Crusader walled town it will be necessary to return via the same route as far as the modern sculpture and then turn right. The coach and car park close to the defensive walls are about 1 km ahead (details of the town on page 189).

After exploring the main ruins of Caesarea continue south along the road running parallel to the sea for about 1 km until reaching the Roman Theatre (details on page 192).

History

In the fourth century BC there was an anchorage here known as 'Strato's Tower', named after the principal landmark. A fortified town subsequently developed which was conquered a number of times before being given to Herod the Great by the Roman Emperor Caesar Augustus in 30 BC. Herod then undertook a most ambitious development which he named 'Caesarea Maritima' in honour of the Emperor. An impressive artificial harbour was constructed capable of providing anchorage for over one hundred ships and this was surrounded by many colonnades and statues. The public buildings included a large theatre, hippodrome, amphitheatre and a Temple to Augustus. It also had a main thoroughfare nearly six metres wide under which was an advanced sewage system flushed daily by sea water. Herod's town was over three times the size of the area now contained within the walls.

During the Roman occupation tensions ran high between Jews and Gentiles. The historian Josephus records that in AD 66, following the desecration of their synagogue, 20,000 Jews were slain and that this massacre was the main cause of the Jewish revolt against Rome. It was from Caesarea that the Roman Emperor Titus set out with his army to sack Jerusalem in AD 70.

In the third century the writer, Origen, who lived in the town for twenty years founded a Christian library and centre of learning here. One of his pupils was Eusebius who became Bishop of Caesarea in AD 314. He was the first church historian and it is due to his records that the position of many biblical sites has been established. At the height of the Byzantine period the town was over eight times the size of the present area, rivalling Jerusalem itself.

After falling into Muslim hands in AD 640, Caesarea declined in importance until the Crusaders captured it in May 1101 and began some redevelopment. However following their defeat by Saladin in 1187 at the Horns of Hattin, the town again changed hands on a number of occasions and it was not until 1251 that some reconstruction, albeit on a much smaller scale, was carried out at the instigation of Louis IX of France. The remains of the large Roman theatre, amphitheatre and hippodrome were not included within the bounds of the town, but his impressive walls and defence ditch, reminiscent of many fortresses in France, are still to be seen.

The French Crusaders were finally defeated by the Marmeluke Sultan, Baybars, only thirteen years after the defensive walls were completed. He destroyed the town which remained unoccupied until 1878 when the Turks allowed a number of refugees from Bosnia to inhabit the site. Their Mosque, a feature of the present tourist area, was in use until this small community abandoned the place in 1948 following the division of the Country by the United Nations. It is only in recent years that Caesarea has been excavated and developed as an attraction for visitors.

Tour

The Crusader walled town: The bridge over the defensive ditch, on the east side of the old town, leads into a covered gateway which is one of the most complete Crusader structures in Israel and reminiscent of many castle entrances in Europe. Pass through the covered gateway and then shortly afterwards turn left to walk through the foundations of various buildings. Notice in particular, lying on the ground immediately to the left of the path, a fine marble Roman column which at some time had a small Christian cross set into it. Ahead are some picturesque arches open to the skies which formed part of a street. It is not difficult to imagine shops on either side similar to the covered Crusader streets in the Old City of Jerusalem. Soon after walking through the arches climb the mound of ruins on the right to reach a plateau where there are further excavations. Continue towards the sea and notice at the highest point the remains of the Crusader Cathedral which was erected on this high ground. The three apses at the east end of the building are clearly recognisable. In fact the cathedral was never completed because the vaults below, from an earlier period, were unable to withstand the weight.

Other features in the attractive area around the harbour are clearly marked and not least the ruins of the Temple which Herod the Great built in honour of Caesar Augustus. Continue along the breakwater to the left and notice how many Roman columns have been used by the Crusaders to reinforce the sea wall. Ahead is a modern restaurant standing upon the remains of a substantial building which was once the Crusader Citadel. Some scholars suggest that this might also have been the site of the Roman prison and if this is correct, then it is likely that here St Paul was detained.

At the time of writing there are extensive archaeological excavations taking place between the Crusader walled town and the Roman Theatre which can be visited if time permits. Some of the main features are now clearly marked.

Authors' Comments

In addition to a wealth of historical interest there are a number of quality shops, restaurants, and also a bathing beach. A relaxing place by the Mediterranean in contrast to the more intense pilgrimage centres of Jerusalem, Nazareth and Galilee.

Opening Times:
April to September: 8.00–17.00
October to March: 9.00–16.00
On the eve of Shabbat and holidays closes 1 hour earlier. Closed on Yom Kippur. Retain the entrance ticket for admission to the remains of the Roman Theatre. The tourist 'green card' is accepted

Souvenir Shop: Many shops within the walls

Toilets: At the far eastern end of the block of shops to the north of the tourist area

Custodian: The National Parks Authority

Telephone: (06) 361358 or (06) 361060

THE ROMAN AQUEDUCT

Access *(see instructions on pages 186 and 188)*

The Aqueduct was built to bring a constant supply of fresh water from the foothills of Mount Carmel into the town. The structure beside the seashore has withstood the onslaught of wind and sand for 2,000 years and still stands as a testimony to the skill of the Roman engineers. There are in fact two aqueducts each with its own water channel and separate foundations. The one nearest to the road was constructed by Herod the Great just before the birth of Jesus, whilst the other nearer the sea was built by Hadrian at the beginning of the second century. The total length of the aqueduct was over twenty kilometres, and for half its distance the water channels were supported on these continuous arches.

There is no admission charge to the area nor any public facilities. Bathing is prohibited because of the dangerous currents.

Biblical References

Acts 8.40: Philip the Apostle reaches Caesarea

Acts 10: Peter comes up from Joppa to baptise Cornelius

Acts 21.8ff: At the home of Philip the Evangelist, Agabus foretells St Paul's treatment in Jerusalem

Acts 23–26: Paul's imprisonment and defence before King Agrippa and Festus.

THE ROMAN THEATRE

Access *(see instructions on pages 186 and 188)*

This impressive structure lies about 1 km to the south of the walled Crusader town. From the ticket office walk diagonally across the sand to the ruins and then pass through one of the archways leading into the tiered auditorium. If there is no wind the acoustic properties can be appreciated and invariably there is someone standing on stage to prove the point. The theatre has a seating capacity of about 4,000 and the rows have been numbered because concerts are occasionally held during the summer months.

Walk down one of the gangways on to the stage, and behind it and on either side will be seen the remains of dressing rooms, rehearsal rooms and other facilities connected with any theatre. Before leaving the site be sure to look at the carvings and statue-remains displayed near the ticket office. Not least

among them is an enormous foot, but more important for the Christian is a replica of part of a carved stone bearing a latin inscription to the effect that: 'Pontius Pilate, Prefect of Judaea, made and dedicated the Tiberieum to the Divine Augustus'. This is positive archaeological evidence to confirm the existence of the Roman Procurator as recorded in the Gospels.

Opening Times:
April to September: 8.00–17.00
October to March: 9.00–16.00
On the eve of Shabbat and holidays closes 1 hour earlier. Closed on Yom Kippur. Retain the entrance ticket for admission to the remains of the walled town. The tourist 'green card' is accepted

Souvenir Shop: Small booth by the ticket office

Toilets: Close to the northern boundary fence between the ticket office and the sea

Custodian: The National Parks Authority

Telephone: (06) 361358

BYZANTINE STREET

If time permits it is worth
visiting another site outside
the walled town. To the east
of the defensive walls, but
south of the road running
away from the gateway, is part
of a **Byzantine street** in
which there are two enormous
statues dating from the second
to third century. The
identification of the one in
white marble has not been
established but the other in
dark granite is thought to
depict the Roman Emperor
Hadrian (AD 76–138) and
may have been carved in
Egypt.

GOSPEL REFERENCES

(The unidentified verses refer to the place name only)

ASCENSION, Place of
Luke 24.50–53   The Ascension
(Acts 1.4–12)   ,,   ,,

BEATITUDES, Mount of
Matt 5.1 to 7.27   Sermon on the Mount
Luke 6.17–49   ,,   ,,   ,,   ,,

BETHANY
Matt 21.17
Matt 26.6–13   Jesus is anointed at Simon the Leper's house

Mark 14.3–9   ,,   ,,   ,,   ,,   ,,   ,,   ,,
Mark 11.1
Mark 11.11–12
Luke 10.38–42   Martha and Mary
Luke 19.29
Luke 24.50
John 11.1–44   Raising of Lazarus
John 12.1–9   Anointing of Jesus by Mary

BETHESDA, Pool of
John 5.2–15   Healing of the paralytic

BETHLEHEM
Matt 2.1–12   Visitation of the Magi
Matt 2.13–15   Joseph's dream and the flight into Egypt
Matt 2.16–18   Massacre of the Holy Innocents
Luke 2.1–20   The Nativity and the story of the Shepherds

John 7.42

BETHPHAGE
Matt 21.1–11   Triumphal entry into Jerusalem
Mark 11.1–11   ,,   ,,   ,,   ,,
Luke 19.28–40   ,,   ,,   ,,   ,,
John 12.12–15   ,,   ,,   ,,   ,,

CAESAREA PHILIPPI
Matt 16.13–20   Peter's commissioning
Mark 8.27–30   Peter's confession of faith

CANA
John 2.1–11   Miracle at the Wedding Feast
John 4.46–53   A healing
John 21.2

CAPERNAUM
Matt 4.18–22   Calling of Peter, Andrew, James and John
Mark 1.16–20   ,,   ,,   ,,   ,,   ,,
Luke 5.1–11   Calling of Peter, James and John
Matt 8.5–13   Healing of the Centurion's servant
Luke 7.1–10   ,,   ,,   ,,   ,,   ,,
Matt 8.14–15   Healing of Peter's mother-in-law

Mark 1.29–34	Healing of Peter's mother-in-law
Matt 8.16–17	Healing of many
Matt 9.1–7	Healing of the Paralytic
Mark 2.1–12	,, ,, ,, ,,
Matt 9.9	Calling of Matthew
Mark 2.13–14	,, ,, ,,
Luke 5.27–28	,, ,, ,,
Matt 9.11–13	Eating with tax-gatherers and sinners
Mark 2.15–17	,, ,, publicans ,, ,,
Matt 9.18–19 & 23–26	Raising of Jairus's daughter
Mark 5.21–24 & 35–43	,, ,, ,, ,,
Luke 8.40–42 & 49–56	,, ,, ,, ,,
Matt 9.20–22	Healing of the woman with haemorrhages
Mark 5.25–34	,, ,, ,, ,, ,, ,,
Luke 8.43–48	,, ,, ,, ,, ,, ,,
Matt 11.23–24	The impenitent town
Matt 17.24–27	Payment of taxes – 'Peter Fish'
Mark 1.21–28	Healing of the demoniac
Mark 9.33–50	The meaning of discipleship
Luke 4.23	
Luke 10.15	
John 2.12	
John 4.46	
John 6.16–71	Teaching

DOMINUS FLEVIT, Church of
Luke 19.41–44	Jesus weeps over the City

EIN KERIM
Luke 1.23–25	John the Baptist is conceived
Luke 1.39–56	Visitation of Mary to Elizabeth
Luke 1.57–80	Birth and naming of John the Baptist

EMMAUS
Mark 16.12–13	Resurrection appearance on the road to Emmaus
Luke 24.13–35	,, ,, ,, ,, ,, ,,

GALILEE, Sea of
Matt 8.23–27	Stilling the storm
Mark 4.35–41	,, ,, ,,
Luke 8.22–25	,, ,, ,,
Matt 14.22–32	Walking on the water
Mark 6.47–51	,, ,, ,, ,,
John 6.16–21	,, ,, ,, ,,
Luke 5.1–11	Catch of fish

GALLICANTU, Church of St Peter in
Matt 26.57–75	Trial before Caiaphas and Peter's denial
Mark 14.53–72	,, ,, the High Priest and Peter's denial
Luke 22.54–71	Peter's denial and trial before The Council
John 18.13–27	Trial before Annas and Peter's denial

GETHSEMANE

Matt 26.36–56	Agony, betrayal and arrest of Jesus
Mark 14.32–50	,, ,, ,, ,, ,,
Luke 22.39–54a	,, ,, ,, ,, ,,
John 18.1–12	Betrayal and arrest of Jesus

HOLY SEPULCHRE, Church of the

Matt 27.33 to 28.10	The Crucifixion and Resurrection
Mark 15.22 to 16.8a	,, ,, ,, ,,
Luke 23.32 to 24.12	,, ,, ,, ,,
John 19.16b to 20.18	,, ,, ,, ,,

JACOB'S WELL

John 4.4–30	Meeting with the Samaritan woman

JERICHO

Matt 20.29–34	Healing of the two blind beggars
Mark 10.46–52	Healing of blind Bartimaeus
Luke 10.25–37	Parable of the Good Samaritan
Luke 18.35–43	Healing of the blind beggar
Luke 19.1–10	Story of Zacchaeus

JORDAN, River

Matt 3.1–12	Baptisms by John
Mark 1.2–8	,, ,, ,,
Luke 3.2–17	,, ,, ,,
Matt 3.13–17	Baptism of Jesus
Mark 1.9–11	,, ,, ,,
Luke 3.21–22	,, ,, ,,

NAZARETH (in chronological order)

Luke 1.26–38	The Annunciation
Luke 2.39–40 & 51–52	Childhood of Jesus
Matt 13.53–58	Teaching in the Synagogue
Mark 6.1–6	,, ,, ,, ,,
Luke 4.16–21	,, ,, ,, ,,
Luke 4.23–30	Jesus is rejected and expelled
Matt 2.23	
Mark 14.67	
John 1.45–46	

PATER NOSTER, Church of

Matt 6.5–15	The Lord's Prayer
Luke 11.1–4	,, ,, ,,
Matt 24 to 25	Jesus foretells the destruction of Jerusalem, and his return in judgement

SILOAM, Pool of

John 9.1–12	Jesus gives sight to a man born blind

SOWER'S BAY

Matt 13.1–9	Parable of the sower
Mark 4.1–9	,, ,, ,, ,,
Luke 8.4–8	,, ,, ,, ,,
Matt 13.18–23	Parable explained

Mark 4.13–20	Parable explained
Luke 8.11–15	,, ,,
Matt 13.24–30	Parable of the wheat and the weed
Mark 4.26–29	,, ,, ,, ,, ,, ,, ,,
Matt 13.31–32	Parable of the mustard seed
Mark 4.30–32	
Matt 13.33	,, ,, ,, ,, ,, Parable of the leaven

TABGHA

Matt 14.13–21	Feeding of the five thousand
Mark 6.30–44	,, ,, ,, ,, ,,
Luke 9.10–17	,, ,, ,, ,, ,,
John 6.1–13	,, ,, ,, ,, ,,
Matt 15.32–39	Feeding of the four thousand
Mark 8.1–10	,, ,, ,, ,, ,,
John 21.1–24	Resurrection appearance including the Commissioning of Peter

TABOR, Mount

Matt 17.1–8	The Transfiguration
Mark 9.2–8	,, ,,
Luke 9.28–36	,, ,,

TEMPLE AREA (in chronological order)

Luke 1.5–25	The Angel Gabriel appears to Zacharias
Luke 2.22–39	Presentation of Jesus in the Temple
Luke 2.41–52	Jesus with the teachers in the Temple
Matt 4.5–7	Temptation – the Pinnacle of the Temple
Luke 4.9–12	,, ,, ,, ,, ,, ,,
Luke 18.10–14	Parable of the Pharisee and the tax collector
Matt 21.12–13	Jesus drives the traders out of the Temple
Mark 11.15–17	,, ,, ,, ,, ,, ,, ,,
Luke 19.45–48	,, ,, ,, ,, ,, ,, ,,
John 2.13–17	,, ,, ,, ,, ,, ,, ,,
Luke 20.1–8	The authority of Jesus
John 2.18–21	,, ,, ,, ,,
John 7.14–52	Teaching
Luke 20.9–16	Parable of the tenants in the vineyard
Matt 21.14–17	Blind and cripples healed in the Temple
Matt 23.38 to 24.2	Destruction of the Temple foretold
Luke 21.5–7	,, ,, ,, ,, ,,
Matt 27.3–10	Judas's remorse
Matt 27.51	The veil of the Temple torn in two
Mark 15.38	,, ,, ,, ,, ,, ,, ,, ,,
Luke 23.45	,, ,, ,, ,, ,, ,, ,, ,,
Luke 23.52–53	The Disciples in the Temple after the Ascension

'UPPER ROOM'

Matt 26.17–30	The Last Supper
Mark 14.12–26	,, ,, ,,
Luke 22.7–38	,, ,, ,,
John 13 to 17	,, ,, ,,

VIA DOLOROSA

Matt 27.1–32	Jesus before Pilate. The Way of the Cross
Mark 15.1–21	,, ,, ,, ,, ,, ,, ,, ,,
Luke 23.1–31	,, ,, ,, ,, ,, ,, ,, ,,
John 18.28 to 19.16a	,, ,, ,, ,, ,, ,, ,, ,,

ZION, Mount. (Traditionally somewhere on the Mount)

Luke 24.36–49	Resurrection appearance to the Disciples
John 20.19–29	,, appearances – 'Doubting Thomas'
(Acts 2.1–47)	Pentecost

FIRST LINES OF HYMNS
Used as Prayerful Thoughts

BIBLIOGRAPHY

Basilica in Nazareth, The. Gumbert Ludwig. 1986
Commissariat of the Holy Land.
Beauty of Jerusalem, The. G. S. P. Freeman-Grenville. 1983.
East–West Publications, London.
Blue Guide to Jerusalem, The. Kay Prag. 1989
A & C Black, London.
Come, see the Place. Ronald Brownrigg. 1985
Hodder and Stoughton, London.
Church of the Holy Sepulchre. Laurence King. 1944
Digging up Jerusalem. Kathleen Kenyon. 1974
Benn, London.
Guide to the Holy Land. Eugene Hoade. 1984
Franciscan Printing Press, Jerusalem.
Holy Land Archaeological Guide, The. Jerome Murphy-O'Connor.
1986
Oxford University Press.
House of St Peter, The. Virgilio Corbo. 1972
Franciscan Printing Press, Jerusalem.
Jerusalem as Jesus knew it. John Wilkinson. 1978
Thames and Hudson, London.
Masada – Herod's Fortress and the Zealot's Last Stand. Yigael
Yadin. 1966
Weidenfeld and Nicholson, London.
Noble Heritage, The. Alistair Duncan. 1974
Longman Group, London.
Pilgrim to the Holy Land. H. J. Richards. 1982
Mayhew McCrimmon, Great Wakering.
Pilgrims to the Holy Land. Teddy Kollek & Moshe Pearlman.
1970
Weidenfeld and Nicholson, London.
Plain Man in the Holy Land, A. James Martin. 1978
St Andrew Press, Edinburgh.

COPYRIGHT ACKNOWLEDGEMENTS

INDEX

(Bold typeface denotes reference to specific sections in the text)